SHOTS IN THE DARK

SHOTS IN THE DARK

JOHN MELLORS

LONDON MAGAZINE EDITIONS 1974

First published in Great Britain 1974
by London Magazine Editions
30 Thurloe Place, S.W.7

SBN 900626 94 1

For Phoebe

Printed in Great Britain
by Billing & Sons Limited, Guildford and London

Contents

Foreword

I don't know whether it is a common reaction for someone who has just written a book to want to review it unfavourably himself. Who is this man, Mellors, I feel like asking, that he should consider these touched-up autobiographical jottings to be of general interest? There seem to me to be only three valid reasons for writing about oneself. A celebrity, even if he is not a writer, is justified in trying to tell how he became a successful composer, chemist, crook or cricketer. Someone quite unknown can have had such a bizarre experience that if he puts it down clearly on paper it will fascinate the rest of us. An accomplished writer can use his own past, however humdrum, and by his creative skill and imagination produce a novel that is a work of art. I do not qualify under any of these headings. What, then, am I up to?

I cannot excuse, but I can perhaps explain. I began by

writing what I hoped would be short stories, based on people and events I remembered from the War; they came out as vignettes, episodic sketches, each too slight to stand on its own. I was then encouraged to regard them as the makings of a book. In working this out I realized that I was mainly interested in extracting the comic element from happenings that had not necessarily struck me as all that comic at the time. This led me to recognize that the emphasizing of the comic was an aspect of my character, a defence mechanism of some kind, a means of ignoring or rejecting what would otherwise terrify, depress or disgust me. I wondered to what extent I had always been like that and how much life in wartime had accentuated what had previously been a less operative trait. And what other alterations and changes of direction had the War brought about in me? To find out, I wrote first about myself before I joined the Army, at home, at school and at Oxford, then about the War, and lastly about the two post-War years when I was at the University again. I behaved very differently when I found myself at Oxford for the second time, five years older. Academic work did not come easily after so long an interval. Oxford with its pubs and girls was a city to be pillaged by men who had been in the Forces longer than they had been undergraduates and who were answerable now to a discipline much more tolerant than that to which they had been subject for several years. If the War had already changed me, then so too did the temptations of post-War Oxford. This, I suppose, is what these recollections are 'about'.

I still think that if *Shots in the Dark* does not work as

comedy, or farce, it does not work at all. I am certainly not trying to prove anything or present a case history. I agree with Hume that to state categorically that one thing has caused another is often presumptuous; usually, all we really know is that something happened and then something else happened. Of course, this attitude suits my idleness. I am a lazy thinker. There are many trails in this book which I have chosen not to follow. Perhaps they will provide me with material for a novel or short stories, if I can bring myself to plan and shape them. Unfortunately, I enjoy writing but not the organizing of what I am going to write.

Finally, not all the events I have described took place in the exact chronological order to which I have assigned them. Some of the people are composite and have been given made-up names and invented physical characteristics. I don't think this makes the book any the less 'true', so long as the reader is not looking for a literally accurate chronicle, which it was never my intention to provide. I have been grossly unfair to parents, some other relatives and several friends, none of whom has deserved such treatment. I have not set out to be malicious (except in a few instances), but it is almost impossible to focus on what is funny in people without distorting them. At least, I hope, I have been equally unfair to myself.

J. M.

A*

Square One

It was when my father encouraged me to walk about the house without shoes on, in order to contract flat feet and so render myself ineligible for the Army, that I began to think his attitude towards the War, or at least to my part in it, was 'a bit off'. We had hardly finished listening to the sad and silly voice of Chamberlain telling us that this country was now at war with Germany before my father rushed me into the town to volunteer for the Royal Navy. "It's a clean life in the Navy, son," he said. "There's no mud on a ship." The recruiting office was shut. "Daft!" said my father. They weren't taking things seriously enough. Why, bombs might rain on Huddersfield at any moment. (Later in the War, when the Blitz was on but Huddersfield remained unbombed, he took it as an insult, a slur upon the town's importance, until he conceived the idea that the Nazis would really like to bomb it but were thwarted by the configuration of the Pennine Hills.) The next day the recruiting office was open, but they told me to go away and wait until I'd had a year at Oxford, they didn't want people as young as me yet. My father suspected that it was all a plot to keep me out of the Navy and get me into the Army when I wasn't looking. As soon as we were back home he told me to take my shoes off. For days I walked about the house in stockinged feet, but except in my father's presence I made a point of walking with a springy step, coming up on to my toes like a demented ballet dancer. Flat feet, whatever they might be, sounded an even more ignominious fate than soldiering.

I had mixed feelings about my father. The two virtues he promoted were honesty and tolerance. This was not a bad programme on the face of it, but he had been thoroughly dishonest to me about sex, even to the extent of denying that there was any difference, physically, between men and women, and his tolerance seemed to be, on the one hand, an excuse for having no very deeply held views, and, on the other, an assumption that family and friends should agree with, indeed admire, his prejudices. I liked him, though, because for summer after summer, until I was about fourteen, he had spent an hour or two most evenings bowling to me with a tennis ball on the asphalt path at the side of the house. As a result, I had an impeccably straight bat, because there was no room to swing it, and an ability to keep the ball down, because if you didn't you almost always broke a window. Unfortunately, it was quite impossible to play any sort of shot on the leg side except the finest glance; if you tried to hook, pull or sweep, you broke the bat against the wall of the next house. At school I got my colours as a correct but painfully slow opening bat, usually able to see off the fast bowlers but almost always out as soon as a slow bowler tempted me to hit to leg.

My father's denial that females were designed any differently from males came when I was nine, after Victor King and I had encountered a strange man on Grimscar Fields. My mother and Mrs King encouraged us to play on Grimscar Fields, where there was nothing more dangerous than the milkman's cows and a shallow stream in which we sometimes got our feet wet. Down in the village among the mills and engineering works there was much to be avoided. Quite often there were outbreaks of diphtheria, and what was called the 'fever van' could be seen waiting outside the rows of workers' cottages. There were certain drains which my mother urged me to walk quickly past, holding my breath and keeping my mouth tight shut, when I went down to the shops for her. I was afraid, too, of something she did not know about, a gang of boys led by one called Rocket in acknowledgement of his sudden bursts of violence. He was particularly skilled at stone-throwing, but once I had cut his knee open when I threw one back. For days I had been in fear, of the police, of Rocket's father, and, most of all, of Rocket himself, but there had been no punishment or retaliation. Grimscar Fields were considered safe, and indeed the man we met there made no effort to molest us; he just described, clearly and in detail, the different construction of women and what happened in the making of babies. To Victor King and me, both 'only' children, it was an eye-opener. I ran home and asked my mother and Aunty Hilda if it was true that they had holes where I had something else. I can't remember what I called a penis then. I was still going to a genteel private school run by an old maiden lady in the local Liberal Club, and I'm sure that words like 'prick' and 'cock' were not yet in my vocabulary.

My mother and aunt were shocked, and my aunt, a spinster, had a fit of the giggles. They said there was no truth in what I had been told and it was very naughty of the man to spread such stories; I must give my father a full account of what had happened when he came home. He listened impassively and then delivered his verdict: "Rubbish!" I questioned him more closely. He conceded a point, about breasts, but continued to deny the more interesting part of the stranger's exposition. He confirmed my mother's view that men like that were wicked and evil, and the following morning Victor King and I were taken to the police station to describe the dangerous wrongdoer.

I knew that my parents were lying and that the man had told the truth. His story was complicated and I didn't entirely follow the mechanics of the operation he had outlined, but I just knew it to be basically true. I never completely believed in my father's honesty again. I continued to trust my mother, oddly enough, since she had in fact been the first to lie; perhaps it was because she had never made such a song and dance about honesty in the first place.

At the same time that I believed the biological facts I had been told on Grimscar Fields, I couldn't really imagine that people I knew, least of all my parents, actually behaved in the way the stranger had described. So I was shocked in my turn when my parents came home late from a dance one night and I heard my father tell my mother a limerick about 'Roger, the lodger, the sod'. It was my mother's laughing at the joke, not the joke itself, that gave the game away. They had lied, they and Victor King's parents, and, for all I knew, everybody's parents, not just about a theory but about a practice in which they themselves indulged.

There was another reason for not valuing too highly my father's advice about war service. He had never been to war. How he had managed to avoid playing an active part in the Great War I never quite fathomed. Both my parents were at pains to conceal a number of important facts about themselves. The difference in their ages, for example: my mother was ten years older than my father, and from their efforts to keep this secret you would have thought they had broken a taboo as strong as incest. Then there was the mysterious disappearance of my paternal grandfather, in whose house we had lived for the first six years of my life. I gathered later, from sources other than my parents, that he had gone off with a barmaid and subsequently married her. This he had been fully entitled to do, as a widower, but it had split the family into those who, like my father, decided to have nothing more to do with him, and those who remained in contact. As a result of this split there were several uncles, aunts and cousins whom I never met. My Aunt Hilda maintained a position of neutrality and succeeded in being persona grata to both parties in the schism.

I had sometimes questioned my father about the Great War, and his answers had left me with the confused impression that not only had he been physically incapacitated by an attack of food poisoning but also was morally disqualified by his intention at that time to go into the Church. He always insisted that he should have gone from school to Oxford, but had been "diddled out of" a scholarship; the form this diddling had taken remained obscure. After reading for the Church in the household of a country vicar in one of the wildest Yorkshire Dales, he had decided against that calling and had taken a job with a Yorkshire colliery, selling their coal on the Manchester Coal Exchange to merchants and factors throughout Lancashire. This enabled him to spend frequent weekends "mixing business with pleasure" in large seaside hotels at Blackpool and St. Anne's, or watching Huddersfield Town play their away games against Bolton Wanderers, Blackburn Rovers and Preston North End, teams in towns where he had his biggest customers. I should think they must have been pretty boozy occasions. Years later, my father advised me what to do about hangovers, admitting that the advice was based on his experiences at places like Cleveleys Hydro and the Majestic in St. Anne's. "Drink a glass of Andrews Liver Salts as soon as you wake up, son. Eat a reasonable breakfast. And then, as quick as you decently can, have a nice cold glass of champagne. You're right as rain in no time."

I wonder now, though I didn't then, if those weekends included women as well as wine, because my father went without my mother more often than she accompanied him. My mother once told someone that a neighbour said to her one day that she had seen my father in Blackpool the previous weekend and that he had been with a woman whom she didn't recognise. My mother said she had refused to let the neighbour continue, and the point my mother was making was that you shouldn't listen to gossip, not that husbands couldn't be trusted.

When I was in my teens I was amused to find that my father kept in a drawer of his desk a copy of *Anna Karenina.* It had been discreetly, if clumsily, jacketed in brown paper, which I took to indicate that this story of adultery had been considered not to be the sort of book that could be left around where wife or son might pick it up. Or perhaps it was the maid he thought Tolstoy might demoralize. We had a succession of maids throughout the 'thirties, all of whom came from a mining village near Barnsley where my mother's eldest brother was a director of two collieries. One girl, I realize now, was a sexy piece. When my mother was out, Dorothy would encourage me to wrestle with her and we always ended up with her on her back and me sitting astride her stomach and bouncing up and down on it. She was about twice as strong as I, so the bouts must have been 'fixed' to end that way. I remember her wriggling and giggling beneath me; an acrid but exciting smell of sweat came from her. I was sorry when she stayed out all one night and my mother sacked her in the morning.

I only really suspected my father of 'carrying on' with women much later, when I came back after the War. He took me once or twice to a pub near the bus terminus on the Bradford Road. The pub had one celebrated customer at that time, the man who had been

Hedley Verity's batman when that hero of my boyhood was killed in the Western Desert. However, I was sure that my father was drawn there not by the witness to the great slow bowler's death, but rather, if the 'nods and becks and wreathed smiles' were anything to go by, to maintain an established liaison with the fat and fortyish barmaid whose black hair, brown eyes and placid disposition kept her still attractive.

I annoyed my father by refusing to join any of the cadet organisations at Oxford. He believed in all forms of insurance and thought I was mad not to pay this premium to make sure of a commission. He was even more annoyed when I joined the Army, not the Navy, in the autumn of 1940. "Daft!" he remarked gloomily. 'Daft' and 'Rubbish' were his favourite words of disapproval. He used them more and more frequently in condemnation of my character and actions as he found I was extricating myself from his sphere of influence. I suppose this process of extrication had started, or at least moved into higher gear, when I went away to school at the age of eleven. He continued, however, to offer me advice at what he called "turning points in life", adopting a solemn expression and prefacing his counsel with "Now son, there are a few important things we ought to talk about." Before I went up to Oxford he urged me to stick to beer and sherry and said he knew I would always "stand my corner". The day I went off to join the Army he produced no memorable maxim but gave me a bottle of Carter's Little Liver Pills and a packet of PK chewing gum.

Confirmation and Coprophagy

Going away to school meant in fact travelling only 15 miles. However, when you slept in a dormitory, and only went home once in thirteen weeks, you might as well have been in Timbuktu. There were forty to fifty boarders in the School House of the Grammar School. The first thing I learned from them was that 'bog' did not mean 'swamp' but 'lavatory'; the second, that the way to succeed with your contemporaries was to make them laugh at your jokes and admire your skill at games. Skill at work was an advantage only in the eyes of the staff, and perhaps a few of the senior boys, and had better be concealed from the rest. This could be done by avoiding mention of Latin, Greek and History classes and making much of abject failures in Algebra and Geometry. "'A long, lean, lanky, lousy-livered lobster!'

he called me, you heard him, didn't you, Ossie?" Also, every now and then it was worth cheeking McBurney to the point of a 'bashing'. McBurney's bashings came only when this otherwise most gentle but ineffectual of masters was goaded into completely losing his temper. He then beat the offending boy about the head, neck and ears with a flurry of blows from the flats of his hands. A 'McBurney bashing' brought great prestige.

It was a highly competitive society, and what each competed for was acceptance and if possible approval by his peers. Livesey could walk on his hands, the whole length of the dormitory. Beverley knew about wireless, and could fix you up with a receiver for listening, headphones under the blankets, to the late-night dance music; Harry Roy was favourite. Steed was the champion farter. After pickled onions or rhubarb had figured on the supper menu, Steed could fart so that the smell was perceptible ten beds away. His most memorable performance was at the end of a day when we had had curry and rice, and then rhubarb, for lunch, baked beans for tea, and bread and cheese and pickled onions, and rhubarb again, for supper. There were enormous fields of rhubarb between Wakefield and Leeds. Real rhubarb addicts maintained that so-called 'French' champagne was in fact made from the pick of the Wakefield rhubarb crop. Others, of whom I was one, suffered greatly during the rhubarb term. It was enough to look at those great bowls of seething, bubbling, pinkish-brown stew for my teeth to be on edge and my stomach shiver. But it did great things for Steed.

However, despite this unique talent, together with a more conventional prowess at rugby and athletics, Steed was not popular. He was feared for being a bully and disliked for his conceit. Even when he was sacked for fucking one of the maids he was not regarded as a hero. The maid, a shy and pretty girl, was sacked too. Her going was deplored, and it was put about that Steed had used his bullying techniques and virtually raped her.

Usually, sexual offences of that order won the offender the awe and admiration of the lesser beings he left behind him. Merryweather, for instance, became a hero overnight. He was a dashing, even swashbuckling youth, densely freckled, with thick, dark hair that he kept well primed with Vaseline. I thought of him as the School House D'Artagnan. He had romantic ideas about girls, insisting that to him it was unbelievable that such beautifully constructed creatures had the same excretory processes as men. "All right, I'll grant you that they pee, that's credible. But shit? You can't really imagine them can you, sitting there crapping the same as us?" I didn't quite know how seriously to take Merryweather's contention, my own knowledge of female anatomy being of the sketchiest and unconfirmed by any experience more direct than hearsay. Merryweather, on the other hand, was said to lead a full sex life and should, therefore, have known all there was to know about the reputedly intricate system of tubes and orifices in the middle of a girl's body. Some remained sceptical of Merryweather's experience until the day he was sacked, when even they could scarce forbear to cheer, he went out in such a blaze of glory. He had entered for some inter-schools boxing tournament, and had been given the key to the gym so that he could train on Sunday afternoons. One Sunday the sports master, unable to find a favourite pipe, thought he might have left it in the gym the previous morning. He found Merryweather and a girl from the town hard at it on the coconut matting. 'A girl from the town' was a particularly emotive phrase. Maids we saw every day. High School girls we saw in church on Sundays and could occasionally talk to. But about 'a girl from the town' there was something indefinably decadent, almost foreign in its naughtiness, as if the female population of Wakefield were made up of artist's models, cancan dancers and prostitutes. Merryweather departed, joined the RAF, and won several decorations during the War. To be fair to the unpopular Steed, he too went into the RAF and had what was known as 'a good war'. The Luftwaffe, I thought later, stood little chance against the sexually precocious drop-outs of the English educational system.

There was, of course, no sex education included in the curriculum of an Elizabethan Grammar School in the West Riding of Yorkshire in the 'thirties. It was said that confirmation classes touched on the subject, and the promise of such instruction led several irreligious but inquisitive fourteen-year-olds to be confirmed in their membership of the Church of England. The classes were a disappointment, and all I can remember of them now is that they were given by a young curate, lately down from Cambridge, who had an impressively exotic name, Dutch-Harrison, in a town where double-barrelled names were a sign of distant origin, and that he told us always to wash our foreskins when we had a bath and not to put brilliantine on our hair before the confirmation ceremony, because the Bishop didn't relish laying his hands on greasy heads. I never went through a religious phase, and when I discovered that attendance at the communion service early on Sunday morning did not mean that the Headmaster would excuse you from having to go to the main morning and evening services, I concluded that confirmation had been a waste of time. One other attempt was made to get me to see the light, on this occasion by a guerilla group, not by the regular forces of the Church. Alec Taylor, a friend of mine at school, was on holiday at Filey with his family when I was there, too, with my parents. All Taylor and I wanted to do was play beach cricket, and we insinuated ourselves one afternoon into a particularly well organized game run by three or four young men, undergraduates probably. One of them invited us both to a 'sausage supper' in a house on The Crescent that evening. It turned out to be rather a dull affair and at about nine o'clock I said I must go back to my hotel. One of the young men asked which hotel this was, and on hearing that it was one on the other side of Filey said he would walk back with me. On the way, he asked me if Jesus had come into my life. No, not really, I said. He stopped, told me to shut my eyes and think hard of Jesus, and then I would see him and he would come into my life. Apart from being highly embarrassing, this was likely to delay my return beyond the hour stipulated by my parents, and if I had to explain the reason I could imagine they'd make a fuss. I was reminded of the time the stranger told Victor King and me the facts of life. There was only one thing to do. After what I judged to be a suitable number of minutes for the apparition of Jesus to arrive, I opened my eyes and said, yes, I had seen him, he had come into my life. The young man seemed pleased and to my relief did not question me about the details of the vision. He made me recite the Lord's Prayer with him and then we parted. I told my parents the sausages had been very nice, fried crisp, the way I liked them. Taylor, I discovered the next day, had been spared a similar performance, because his hotel was only a few doors away from the young men's house. Their tactics had evidently been to accompany those who had a fair walk home.

During an earlier holiday in Filey I had made friends with a girl on the sands. She had long blonde plaits and showed promise as a beach cricket wicketkeeper. Her father was a parson, but he didn't wear a dog-collar, at least not on holiday. When we got back to Foords Hotel one morning before lunch she and I were told to go to the bathroom and wash the sand off our legs. My father drew me on one side. "Don't take your trousers off in front of Margaret, will you, son?" As we sat on the side of the bath, dangling our legs in the water, it occurred to me that here was an opportunity to check on the female characteristics the stranger had informed me of and on which my father had commented: "Rubbish!" I couldn't think how to go about it. Strip off first and ask her to do the same? I hadn't the nerve. Ask her to take her knickers off? Unthinkable! By this time she was drying her feet and the opportunity had passed.

Three times in the 'thirties I went on walking tours in Germany. The first time I put my foot on the quay at Ostend I felt an excitement that religion had failed to give me. Unlike Jesus, 'abroad' had come into my life and was always to attract me, even in the Army, even on routine business trips. The trains had blue lights and wooden seats; the engines gave high-pitched screams. Station signs said Liège and Aachen. The youth hostels were full of Hitler Jugend. By day they marched, like an army, singing the Horst Wessel and other rousing songs, while we ambled, straggled, feeling at first ashamed, then what the hell, who did they think they were, this wasn't the army, we were on holiday. In the evenings, sitting in the dark, soft warmth, high above the Rhine, they played guitars and sang 'Wilde Gesellen' and other romantic ballads. Our master in charge said we had to sing something in return and we gave them a halfhearted rendering of 'On Ilkla Moor baht 'at'. The mädchen wore skimpy white blouses, more like vests, tee shirts they would now be called, embroidered with red swastikas; their big breasts wobbled as they walked. At night there was a lot of giggling and squealing in the girls' dormitory, and the older boys in our party said the German boys were encouraged to sleep with the girls and produce babies to swell the numbers of the Herrenvolk. I said I thought they were supposed to be short of lebensraum. Dawson, the Head Boy, said they'd be far shorter after what was going on next door in the liebensraum. When we were in Bavaria Hindenburg died, and the waitress in a village café was weeping as she served us; our master said she had told him that now there was nobody to stop Hitler from doing exactly as he liked. Coming back through the Black Forest most of us were running out of money. We had been eating a lot of fruit tarts and drinking beer and cherry brandy; Blake held the record for fruit tart, seven large sections of peach flan at one sitting. Marsden had only a few pfennigs left. He was frantic. Ossie still had quite a lot of money and said he'd give Marsden five marks if he ate an inch of his own shit without being sick. Several of us said we'd chip in with a mark each, too. In a café lavatory, with Ossie and one other witness, Marsden managed it. One minute's successful coprophagy changed the balance of power in the party. For the last day or two, while the rest of us drank beer or apfelsaft, Marsden flaunted exotic drinks like Danziger Goldwasser; two little bits of what looked like gold leaf lay at the bottom of the glass and bubbles went slowly up from them through the clear liquid. Marsden let me have a sip, but I can't remember now what it tasted like.

By the time of the third and last of these trips I was in the Sixth and a member of the Left Book Club. Three or four others were fellow-travellers in the political sense, too. If we saw a 'Juden Unerwunschtete' notice in a café, we made a point of getting up from our table, going over to it and reading it slowly, shaking our heads, and then ostentatiously leaving. Our master met a German schoolmaster he knew and left us in his charge for a day. "This morning," said the German, "we will form up in a column and march properly." He got about half the party to do this and the rest of us slouched along in an even more slovenly way than usual, hands in pockets or swishing at the grass with our sticks, and whistling 'The Red Flag'. He was furious and denounced us vehemently to our master on his return. I was sorry for him on reflection; it was probably quite dangerous for him to be noticed in charge of such an unruly mob. We behaved deliberately badly throughout the fortnight. From the tower of a modern youth hostel on the shore of the Bodensee we spat foaming gobs of Fruit Salts on to dustbins far below; bewildered Hitler Youth searched the sky for ailing storks. We went out for a drink one evening and returned to the Jugendherberge a few minutes after its official closing time. In the lighted doorway we could see the Hausvater waiting with our master, so we reeled drunkenly and sang 'By the light of the silvery moon'. When anyone said "Heil Hitler" to us we responded with "Gruss Gott". It must have been largely thanks to our master's tact that none of us got into more than temporary trouble. I brought back some good German editions of Homer and Horace, and a thin selection of Baudelaire which I'm sure Hitler didn't know was still on sale in the Reich.

The next year Eggleshaw, the senior classics master, took Elliott and me to Provence. "Paris, Lyon, Méditerranée!" sang the porters, and it was the song of freedom. We sat outside the Palais des Papes in Avignon reading *L'Humanité*, eating enormous pâté sandwiches and drinking Chateauneuf. Café floors were thick with Gauloise stubs and the trains didn't always run to time. Roman amphitheatres towered over the less ancient buildings round them. In Yorkshire they took you to a field and said, "See that strip of grass a different colour from the rest? That's where a Roman pipeline ran!" In Nîmes and Arles and Orange the most impressive buildings were Roman, and the Roman lavatories at Vaison looked in better shape than those in the hotel where we were staying. Latin seemed not such a dead language, after all.

I had become, for ever, I think, pro-French and anti-German. It was difficult to visit Hitler's Germany in one's mid-teens and be anti-Nazi without being anti-German, and to be aware of the origin and unfairness of a prejudice does not mean one can eradicate it. Even in 1970, after a week's not unpleasant holiday in Germany, to cross into Alsace and sit in a rather dilapidated café, where my wife, returning from the lavatory, was slapped on the bum and asked her views on the best way of cooking haricots verts, was like returning to the Promised Land.

Turpe Nescire

Taking a scholarship exam in the hall of Queen's, I hated the candidate sitting opposite. He had spiky hair and thick-lensed spectacles. As soon as a paper was put in front of him, he read it greedily, smiling and snorting with delight; then he wrote, solidly, without a pause, grunting for joy every now and then, to the very last moment of each 3-hour period. On the third day my feelings towards him had become murderous and of my own chances I had despaired. The next week I learned that I had got a scholarship and he hadn't.

My friend Elliott had so far been unsuccessful, and in February the Head told me to go away with him for a week's holiday. We decided to spend it writing a novel in, and about, a big resort in the off-season. We went to Blackpool. Our style turned out to be much like that of Stevie Smith in *Novel on Yellow Paper*. There was nothing you could call a plot. Characters had names like 'the

Edna Best barmaid' and 'the convalescing miner'; they gave their opinions about each other's opinions on sex, unemployment and the Spanish Civil War. A few weeks later Elliott sat for another scholarship, at Univ., and got it. We sent the manuscript of our novel to Roger Sharrock, who was already up at St. John's, so that the ground could be suitably prepared for the authors' arrival in Oxford in the autumn, but he lost it and we didn't have a copy. (Elliott and Sharrock were my closest friends at school. Elliott went into the RAF and was killed. Roger Sharrock, with whom I am still friendly, is now a don, editor and critic.) We didn't mind the loss too much, because by then we had contacted the local Communist Party and our mentor was no longer Stevie Smith but John Strachey. We sat plotting in a pub called the 'Number 20 Vaults'; it was near the school, but sufficiently dirty and dismal never to attract the masters' custom. On a wall in the abominably smelly lavatory was written: "I would like to touch Alice Faye's thighs". We convinced ourselves that the anonymous author, certainly working-class, probably unemployed, had produced one of the greatest lines of romantic literature, comparable in power to the couplet in Racine which had caused Alfred de Musset to faint in his box at the theatre, although there was no evidence that anyone suffered a similar effect in his stall in the dank grotto behind the 'Number 20 Vaults'.

We were never good at being communists, although I continued to 'fellow-travel', more and more half-heartedly, to the end of my first year at Oxford. I don't think, though, that at the time we took up communism we were altogether wrong or irresponsible in supporting the C.P. When the Government had, to say the least, a wishy-washy attitude to Hitler, Mussolini and Franco, the more 'bite' and organization there was in the anti-fascist movement the better, and the communists were certainly the best organized and probably the most determined in their opposition to the dictators—at any rate before the German–Soviet pact. What infuriated me most was the patronizing opinion that every young man had to go through a period of idealism, e.g. communism, before graduating to common sense. My father resorted to this view after his first assaults of "Daft!" and "Rubbish!" However, after the early excitement of being introduced into something known as a 'cell' and to people who called one another 'comrade', it began to get rather boring. All those damned pamphlets. And while there were plenty of left-wing writers to admire, like Orwell and Auden, the hard-line communists themselves tended to be both humourless and inelegant. As for the communist classics, Marx and Lenin, at least in translation, were tedious in the extreme. I led a kind of double life, I suppose, one evening agreeing that nothing mattered except in so far as it helped to strengthen the revolution that had already taken place and hasten the other revolutions that hadn't yet but undoubtedly would, the next venturing further and further into the 'temps perdu' of Proust, where nothing mattered except in so far as it provided material for the artist to recollect and by his genius transform.

Moreover, Marxists were not expected to have romantic love affairs, and I was constantly having them, not even with 'real people', but with characters I met in books and films. There was Rosie in *Cakes and Ale*. Isherwood's Sally Bowles. Madeleine Carroll, to whom Robert Donat actually lay handcuffed on a bed in *The 39 Steps*. Ginger Rogers. Ginger Rogers? I can't think why. Her skirts swirled magnificently as she and Fred Astaire leaped on and over furniture and up and down staircases, but could that have been enough?

I could identify with Julien in his infatuation with Madame de Rênal in *Le Rouge et le Noir*, in fact I thought Stendhal was the first novelist with a completely modern hero. I couldn't identify with Swann, so I never fell in love with Odette, although I felt a sentimental affection for the belle époque in which she and her cattleyas so exotically flowered. My grandest passion was for Catherine in *A Farewell to Arms*, and it was a passion from which I never fully recovered. All through the War I hankered after finding myself in a military hospital with a not too serious wound (and not too painful, either; identification with Lieutenant Henry could go too far) which a Catherine-type nurse would dress tenderly, falling in love with me in the process. The nearest I got to this ideal was when I had malaria. A big blonde nurse called Olga seemed rather keen on me, but she expressed it by waking me up in the mornings with a cold sponge on the back of my neck. My reaction sent her into fits of laughter. One night when I was over the fever she asked me to accompany her to her quarters when she went off duty. Halfway there she stopped, sighed, looked up at the sky and asked me if I knew any poetry. Despite her name, she had a broad

Geordie accent. I followed her gaze to the bright tropical stars and quoted: "Up above the world so high, like a teatray in the sky." She didn't ask me in for coffee.

Having acquired my scholarship almost at the beginning of my last school year, I was able to devote twelve whole months to reading what I wanted. I listened to a lot of music, too. An indulgent Headmaster allowed me to go to concerts in Leeds and Bradford on Saturday nights. He even saw that cold meat and a bottle of beer were left ready for my return. Barbirolli conducted the Northern Philharmonic in Leeds Town Hall, his black hair flapping up and down. In St. George's Hall, Bradford, I sat level with Beecham conducting Mozart; he ate sweets, sang, and shouted at the orchestra. Some Saturdays I went with Elliott, who was a dayboy, to a greyhound stadium. Elliott had a system, to make us rich. It involved betting on 'forecasts', i.e. forecasting the first and second dogs, out of about six, in each race. We won for a week or two, and then lost it all. There was an additional hazard for me, because on Sunday mornings I had to describe to the Head concerts I hadn't been to. One holiday Elliott and I went to London. In the afternoon we saw a dog called Roeside Creamery break the track record at Stamford Bridge. From there we went to Covent Garden where Baronova danced the Firebird. There was a balletic quality about greyhound racing, we decided. Kennel lads wearing white coats and either bowlers or straw boaters paraded the dogs before each race. The procession would stop and wait reverently when a dog wanted to relieve itself; as the column moved off again a man rushed out with a brush and pan to clear the track. After each race, seedy and raffish-looking men, fugitives from a Graham Greene novel, ceremoniously swore and tore up wads of tote tickets.

I wrote a story for the school magazine in which I described a woman in a bar wearing "a tight yellow jumper over rubber-jumping breasts". It was put to me that this would be less likely to cause offence if I would change 'breasts' to 'breast'. I refused, and won my point. I, as Head Boy, and two other prefects who were also leaving, had to choose, learn and recite on our last Speech Day passages from Eng. Lit. I chose something from Auden which included the lines:

"It's better to sit down to nice meals than to nasty,
It's better to sleep two than single,
It's better to be happy."

There was a row about this, too, but since the Headmaster was retiring at the end of the term, and it was his last Speech Day as well as mine, there was a somewhat relaxed atmosphere and I got my way again.

The Head was a charming man, in fact. He sang the Odes of Horace to a tune of his own devising, to ram home the metre. I can still sing his version of 'O fons Bandusiae, splendidior vitro'. He was a keen fives player and some of us were adept at using the pepper pot to deflect the ball on to his bald head. At night, after prayers, he would often suggest playing billiards with me on his three-quarter-size table. He had a large scrapbook which he used for evening prayers. It contained passages from Dante, Milton, Tennyson (he particularly liked the lines about Ulysses' mariners "That ever with a frolic welcome took/The thunder and the sunshine and opposed/Free hearts, free foreheads"), gnomic utterances of a 'Confucius he say' style, such as "If every man swept his own doorstep, the city would soon be clean", and instances of intellectual courage, his favourite being Zola's *J'Accuse*. Sometimes he didn't even use his scrapbook and just reminisced. "Oliver St. John Gogarty popped up beside me in the water and said, 'For the love of God, Spilsbury, do you have a safety-pin on you? Me bathing drawers is falling off!' Very Irish, you see, the assumption that I would be carrying safety-pins, bathing in the Aegean! In the name of the Father and the Son and the Holy Ghost, Amen—well, Mellors, shall we knock the balls about a bit?" This was a bore on nights when I had a Greek or Latin Prose to finish, and called for careful tactics. If he won the first game that would most likely be enough. If I won it he was certain to propose "best of three, I think, don't you?" He had been Head at Wakefield for about twenty years, but he once told me that the first time he had encountered a Yorkshireman had been when he was a freshman at Queen's and had sat next to a man in Hall who said to the scout: "Ah'll tek th' Eyetalian cootlet". Spilsbury taught Homer, Virgil and Horace in a delightfully dilettante way, as headmasters in their mid-sixties are entitled to do, I think. The real powerhouse on the classical side was the Classical Sixth Formmaster, Eggleshaw, It was he who decided that certain people were good enough to win Oxford scholarships, and he gave them enough individual attention and extra tuition, without extra payment, of course, to see that they did win them. He took Elliott and me to Provence. He made everyone in the form write a fortnightly essay on a book of his, the boy's, own choice. I can remember a definite stage, almost an exact date, when I could no longer be bothered with Galsworthy and Hugh Walpole and began choosing Aldous Huxley, James Joyce and T. S. Eliot; it was like reaching a literary puberty. He organised play readings: Shaw, O'Neill, Giraudoux. He lent us books and records. Swooped on clichés and sloppy thinking. Advised us to trust nobody, except possibly Bertrand Russell and Koestler. He worked extremely hard at helping to civilize as many people as he could.

The school was academically élitist—in sport, too, of course—but socially as free of class discrimination as an English community can ever be. There were sons of labourers and lawyers, miners and colliery managers, lock-keepers and professional cricketers and commercial travellers. Under Spilsbury, boys on local grants were encouraged to enter the Sixth even when it was pretty certain that they would only be there one year and would therefore not be taking Higher School Certificate before going into clerical or what would be called 'working class' jobs at the age of sixteen. I should think the 'class breakdown' in the school was at least 80% working to 20% middle class. Boarders were almost all from the 20%. It was completely intolerant of whatever heterosexual escapades were discovered, to the point, almost always, of expelling the offender; punished, though not all that severely, instances of homosexuality; and allowed most non-sexual eccentricities to flourish. Maurice Hyde was at one and the same time a Mosleyite and an admirer of Haile Selassie; he had a blackshirt uniform and a replica of the Lion of Judah's cloak, scarlet-lined and fastened by a chain. He was a harmless exhibitionist, a nut, and treated affectionately as such even by anti-fascist contemporaries and staff.

Classics and rugby football were the school's main strengths. It was rugby mad. A scrum-machine stood at the side of the pavilion like a shrine, and it was worshipped most afternoons or evenings during the Michaelmas and Easter terms. One of my unhappiest memories is of captaining the 2nd XV in a match at Harrogate when we lost a centre with a broken leg in the first five minutes and were beaten by over thirty points. All the way back in the coach, Clayton's plaster-encased leg stretched on the back seat, not much heart in the singing, I wondered how I could ever live down such an ignominious defeat.

There had been a classics tradition probably since the foundation in the XVIth Century and certainly since the great XVIIth Century scholar, Bentley, had been at the school. I wouldn't dream of defending a classical education to the extent of suggesting that Greek and Latin should be put back in those curricula from which it has been dropped. For one thing, classics is a very time-consuming subject and not susceptible to short cuts and crash courses. It doesn't really become worthwhile until after the 'A' level (old Higher School Certificate) stage, but then it does contribute to Sprachgefühl and the capacity to enjoy words being tellingly and economically used both in one's own and other languages. It can bear fruit in the oddest fields. I would even say it was a good preparation for a career as an advertising copywriter if I didn't mind having 'parturiunt montes et nascitur ridiculus mus' thrown at me.

A few boys succeeded in going up to a university to read maths or science, but there always seemed to be the impression that they could have brought more credit to the school and to themselves if their talents had not been diverted into these interesting but ultimately less important byways. Of course, any form of learning was better than ignorance. After all, the school's motto was 'Turpe Nescire', and one of the Head's favourite quotations a line from Goethe, 'Es ist immer gut etwas zu wissen'. But there were grades of knowledge, and the physics master had to know his place. History was on the way up: a new master, who looked like Lord Peter Wimsey and had in fact been seen at the theatre wearing tails, was going great guns. English, however, was still not regarded as a subject in its own right, despite Eggleshaw's innovations in the Classical Sixth; it was necessary for the General Paper in scholarship exams, and desirable if you were going to lead a fully cultivated life, but boys were not encouraged to aim at entrance to a university in order to read English. Roger Sharrock was the only boy I can remember getting either a scholarship or exhibition in English, and I don't think the school contributed much towards his success. At least they recognised his calibre and let him get on with his reading on his own. They even had the grace to excuse him games; I think that in fact a school which took rugby and cricket so seriously just couldn't bear to see Roger's pathetic attempts to manipulate a moving ball, and it was probably a decision based more on aesthetics and self-interest than on a reasoned judgment of what was best for him.

It is fashionable now to look back on school as the unhappiest days. Even with my facility for remembering the good and dismissing from my memory the bad, I cannot feel that way. Of course there were miseries. Sunday afternoons when all junior boarders were forced to go for long walks: cold grey slabs of winter boredom by the undistinguished banks of the Calder when I wanted to sit by a fire and read Conan Doyle's *The White Company* or Baroness Orczy's *The Scarlet Pimpernel.* The agony of wrestling with stud, stiff collar and tie on freezing Sunday mornings before church. Being thrown in to that vile chlorine-scented water in the baths. All one terrible term, trying to conceal that the dentist had put some contraption behind my front teeth to push them forward; I had to go every week for him to tighten up what looked like minute pegs but felt in my mouth like enormous instruments of torture. However, these instances were all in my first two or three years. Things got better all the time, and I thoroughly enjoyed the last four or five years. Being encouraged to read novels, plays and verse and write essays about them, trained to handle Greek and Latin to a degree of competence when you can begin to appreciate the vivacity and flexibility of the one and the compression, strength and resonance of the other, and every now and then on the cricket field timing a stroke so rightly that you know you're going to make runs—there are worse times in life. Even some of the food wasn't bad. Potato cakes with bacon for breakfast. Stewed rabbit with forcemeat balls for lunch every other Sunday. Treacle tart on Saturdays: though, sometimes, the Head would say, "Playing this afternoon, Mellors? Then I'm not going to offer you a second helping."

Education Sentimentale

I never—at least, not consciously, I suppose I had better add—wanted another boy sexually, and, so far as I could tell, no boy lusted after me. I think I was a late developer and for that reason missed the homosexual phase. Some boys had what seemed like real love affairs. They teased, flattered, scolded, wept, and went to each other's beds after lights-out; sometimes I could hear them whispering, and the bedclothes rustling, but it was even more impressive when they just lay together, silent, motionless. Then there were those who wanted only a quick bang with whoever was willing to reciprocate. I came across Boyd and Vorster in the showers one day, their blue running shorts round their ankles, standing there tossing each other off. They appeared to be enjoying it, but to me they looked ridiculous. For one thing, Boyd was a big, tall chap, good at games. Vorster was short and fat and not good at anything. His parents owned a circus and Vorster's home was a caravan, a most luxurious one, according to his description. Certainly his mother, a fat, overdressed lady, gave every appearance of being rich. She came some weekends in a large, chauffeur-driven car to take Vorster out to a huge tea of egg, sausages and chips, followed by waffles with maple syrup. Mr. Vorster, whom I never saw, was a South African. I didn't think Boyd and Vorster were doing anything wrong. I just didn't want to do it myself, and it looked so silly. Wet dreams, on the other hand, were enjoyable, quite private, and occurred often enough, spontaneously. It didn't seem to me, when I was thirteen and fourteen, that anything else was necessary.

I imagine that homosexual activities were confined almost entirely to boarders. We had all the opportunities for them, and almost none for doing anything with girls. Only those of great initiative and determination, like Steed and Merryweather, achieved anything in that direction. Dayboys, though, were always meeting girls, and their evenings and weekends were not subject to the same ascetic discipline as ours. When I was sixteen I was provoked by a dayboy into accepting a challenge and a bet that immediately I feared were beyond my powers of audacity and ingenuity. Before the end of term, five weeks away, I was to handle a certain High School girl's breast, in front of witnesses. Five shillings were at stake. The girl, of course, was not to know about the wager; it would have been too easy to have taken her into my confidence and split the winnings. I decided that the only place where my caress would be accepted by the girl and could be observed by the appointed witnesses was in a cinema.

I forget the girl's name, but I know it was one I didn't like: Elsie? Edna? Agnes? I had seen her once or twice. She was pretty, rosy-cheeked with dark, curly hair and a well developed figure. There would be no difficulty in discerning the objective, and the challenger had generously allowed me to attempt either side. I sent a note by a dayboy who lived near her. I had admired her from afar, I wrote; would she come with me to the pictures the Saturday afternoon after next? I had had to study rugby fixtures carefully and make sure I would not be playing, even in a practice match. Going to the cinema without permission was something I would just have to risk. Permission was only given when parents or relations were taking you out, or on the extremely rare occasions when the film was considered educational, like George Arliss's 'Disraeli'. The go-between brought back her acceptance.

I had, in fact, neglected to find out what film was being shown that afternoon. I had worried a lot, usually in bed at nights, about the several stages of the operation. If I was not to be rejected at the critical moment I would have to gain her confidence and assure her that my intentions were, if not honourable, at least sincere and motivated by admiration and desire. This, I reasoned, would have to be achieved mostly by looks and gestures. There would be little opportunity for words, nor did I feel up to using them. The penultimate move, I reckoned, would be the holding of her hand. In all this I had assumed I would be helped by the visual images before us and the background music. Unfortunately, the film turned out to be a Will Hay comedy, set in, of all places, a school. Not only was the mood all wrong, there were physical difficulties, too. The girl found the film extremely funny and showed her appreciation by rocking backwards and forwards in her seat, raising her hands to the level of her shoulders and then at the climax of a joke clapping them together soundlessly. She was never still. I was beginning to despair of ever satisfying the two observers sitting in the row behind, when, after one particularly frenzied reaction to the antics of the disreputable master, she brought her right hand down with a thwack on to my left thigh and kept it there. I covered it with my right hand, and the next time she rocked forward moved my left hand round her neck and on to the objective but outside her clothes. To my amazement she allowed this liberty, seeming indeed to encourage it by moderating her movements and inclining towards me. Two or three blouse buttons and a couple of layers of cloth were all that stood between me and victory. Not being left-handed, I found the buttons difficult. She undid one herself. Cautiously, I slid my fingers in. I was there! A witness tapped me on the shoulder and asked for a match, the signal that my feat was recognised, the wager won. Thankfully, I withdrew my hand. The girl put it back. I kept it there, thinking it would be rude now to withdraw it, until just before the lights went up. I took her home, talking about the film, and kissed her on her doorstep. It was the least I could do, I thought, and, for that matter, the most. I didn't take her out again. I had received no sexual thrill at all, merely relief at enduring an ordeal and meeting a challenge. It was like not shirking a tackle or backing away to square leg. Of course, I had to give a different account of matters when questioned by my challenger. Did I get a hard on? Oh yes, I said, she was hot stuff. Did her nipple get a hard on? I hadn't known that nipples could, but yes, I said, it did, no trouble at all, the very first moment that I touched it.

After being introduced to France by Eggleshaw, I went again, with Elliott, Blake and Marsden, and no accompanying master, this time to Paris. Elliott had a friend, a bank clerk, who had 'done' Montmartre, and from him we had a list of places worth a visit. We picked up four American girls at the American Express and offered to escort them round Paris by night. We went to the first place on the list, Chez Eve. It was all right, a bare-breasted chorus line, some Apache dancers and a contortionist. It was, in fact, exactly what the girls had wanted to see. They could regard it as naughty, a bit of 'Gay Paree', although really it was a slick but innocuous tourist show. One snag, from our point of view, was the cost; for example, they only served champagne. Fortunately, the girls had plenty of money. They were from one of those schools or colleges like Vassar or Wellesley that even we had heard of. They insisted that they would pay their share.

We moved on to address number two on our list. It was an anonymous-looking establishment, bleak and uninviting. No neon lights, no commissionaire. The driver of the taxi I was in had seemed surprised at our choice of destination. We went in. There was a small lobby and then one immense room, brightly lit, with round café tables and plain wooden chairs, and a bar running the length of one side-wall. A short, fat, elderly woman in black led us to the middle of the room and pushed one table up against another to accommodate us. We sat down, none of us prepared to reveal surprise or embarrassment that the woman in black was the only one out of some twenty or thirty women to be wearing any clothes at all, unless you counted necklaces and high-heeled evening shoes. The dozen or so men who sat at tables, or stood at the bar, drinking with and talking to their naked companions were all fully, and indeed soberly, dressed, even, in some cases, to the point of continuing to wear their hats. Against the back wall, the unoccupied women stood chatting and laughing among themselves.

Elliott ordered beer all round. Four women detached themselves from the group at the back and joined us. Beer was brought for them as well. Madame hovered nearby, frowning suspiciously. I wondered if we should attempt to explain to her why we had brought our own young, attractive and respectably dressed girls with us, but there seemed no explanation possible that would not appear rude either to the organization that was receiving us or to the Americans we were escorting. The whores, as I now presumed they were, told us their names, asked where we came from, accepted cigarettes. I introduced the one on my left to the American girl on my right The woman reached across me and shook hands politely, her left breast swinging against my beer and nearly knocking it over. More beers came. The conversation flagged. The women looked expectant,

Madame rather cross. I had never seen a woman naked before and now here was a room full of them, one actually at my elbow talking to me. I was surprised how many of them had ginger pubic hair, even when the hair on their heads was of a different colour. Women, I thought, looked much bigger and more impressive without their clothes on. The Vassar girls, indeed, appeared to have shrunk and their social aplomb quite to have deserted them. I noticed the one next to me staring with some horror at a couple standing at the bar. Talking animatedly, each with a glass in one hand, the man with his trilby pushed to the back of his head, they might have been any couple anywhere, except that the woman was stark naked and had unbuttoned the man's fly and put her free hand inside. I wondered if this was the before or after treatment.

We left after the second round of drinks. Madame shrugged, as if now she had seen everything. The women shook hands again, politely, charmingly. They were attractive, most of them, and I was sorry to go, but we couldn't very well ask the American girls to leave. We walked off to find a taxi. One of the Americans said, well, that was quite something, she guessed they'd be the only girls in their party to have been taken to a place like that. "You boys certainly know your way around." We accepted without protest this undeserved compliment, but we judged that if ever the evening had held any romantic potential, it had now been dissipated. We said goodbye to the girls outside their hotel. They were leaving for Italy the next day. We had to go back home, we decided the next morning. We'd forgotten to take up the girls' offer to go Dutch, and we'd spent three or four days' money in one night. Marsden was most despondent. He'd planned a second, more purposeful, visit to the brothel.

In the Easter holidays, the last before the War, I went to the Lake District with my cousin Enid. We stayed in a boarding house in a place called Seascale, on the coast, near to where she'd been at school. The idea was to play golf. Enid was about ten years older than I. When I'd been small my parents had made me call her 'Aunty Enid', but from as far back as I could remember I'd regarded her as a glamorous figure, and in my teens I felt towards her something of the not quite real romantic yearning that I felt towards certain heroines of films and fiction. She had been what was known as a Bright Young Thing, I suppose, and at one time had sported an Eton crop. She smoked cigarettes in a long holder, swore, had many men admirers, drove, dashingly, a bull-nosed Morris, drank dry martinis, and was good at golf and tennis. She was pretty, with fair hair and blue eyes. She laughed a lot.

My uncle, her father, was a rich coalowner. He had a large house near Barnsley with a big garden, a tennis court, a paddock, in which pit ponies sometimes grazed, and a rookery. There were always lots of dogs, little dogs like Cairns and West Highlanders for the house, and gun dogs who were kept in kennels by the garage. He had two cars (not counting Enid's) and a chauffeur. Most awe-inspiring of all, he had a butler called Fish. Fish was hunchbacked and had very red hands. I got on rather well with my uncle. He had a sardonic sense of humour. My aunt was quick-tempered and behaved like a dowager duchess. She strutted rather then walked. As if powered by some automatic mechanism, she would always stop about two feet short of a door, not turning or standing aside but staring fixedly at it, until a male or servant or, failing them, one of her own three daughters dodged round to open it for her. She had been a primary schoolteacher, I think, before marrying my uncle. After a drink or two her sharp tongue could be entertaining, and she had an earthy laugh, but I always felt I had to mind my ps and qs and be quick to open those doors.

Enid's eldest, unmarried, sister was well read. Enid was not, though she had heard of most of the modern authors I was reading. I let her down badly one day at her local golf club. She introduced me at tea to one of her friends, a petite, dark, beautifully pearled and twin-setted lady, and said I read a lot. Who is your favourite author, I was asked. Instead of giving the name of someone I genuinely admired, I tried to guess what writers the lady herself would like. I'd summed her up as 'Golf Club' and I thought her reading was probably limited to thrillers and detective stories. "Agatha Christie," I said wildly. Interesting, the lady commented, and changed the subject. Driving home, Enid said I was an idiot and had made her look one, too; her friend read poetry and went often to the theatre in Leeds and London.

One reason for the golfing holiday at Seascale was that I had had a knee injured during the rugby season and wanted to give it a good work-out before my last cricket term at school. After a day's golf on the windy links we ate high tea in our boarding house and then walked down to the one hotel for a drink. One night I drank gin and ginger beer and we walked back arm in arm in the dark. I got an erection and I was scared she'd notice in the house, so I said good night quickly and went to bed. By the time I had put on my pyjamas it had gone down. I could decently approach Enid. I had a vague intention of getting into bed with her. We were going back to Yorkshire the next day. It was now or never. I knocked at her bedroom door and went in. She was sitting up in bed brushing her hair. I couldn't think how to go about it. Once she'd been 'Aunty Enid'; she was certain to reject me, and probably she'd laugh. I said I'd run out of handkerchiefs. I borrowed one of hers and went back to my room.

Reviews and Interviews

It was difficult finding my way about Oxford in 1939, literally, because of the blackout and the piles of sandbags in unexpected places, metaphorically, because of the assumption that freshmen should know who was who and what was what even if nothing was explained. That lordly figure in the grey chalk-stripe suit strolling through the Front Quad, if he wasn't the Provost he must be someone almost equally important. When I saw him that night in Hall, serving dinner with the other scouts, I went hot and cold at the thought of the many pitfalls awaiting the unwary.

The Isis had closed down, I think 'for the duration', but Elliott and I each did a film review for *The Cherwell*. Mine was in a suburban cinema miles down the Cowley Road. I'd never watched a film so intently. Half way through, people sniffed uneasily, as if the cinema were on fire, but it was only my left trouser leg that I'd started burning with a cigarette. *The Cherwell* took us both on. The editor was genial and free from the affectations of the literary set, but some of the contributors behaved like nineteenth century dandies. One arrogant young man, who in face and build closely resembled Oscar Wilde, was a master of the crushing phrase and dismissive look. He wore fur waistcoats, never, it seemed, the same one twice. I disliked him intensely because he made me feel so small. Then, at a sherry party one Sunday morning in Magdalen, he said he considered my poem to be the best thing in the current issue. Instantly, I knew him for a perceptive critic, a man of sound judgment and good taste, and, indeed, a rather pleasant chap when you saw beyond the poseur. I had been reading Elizabeth Bowen's *Death of the Heart*, and my poem began: "The heart has died indeed/And the will is only a will/Not to notice death." I cannot remember any specific event which could have given rise to such statements, but there was a strange Jahresgeist in Oxford that first year of the War; sometimes it provoked gloom and despondency, sometimes a hectic, 'live now, pay later' attitude. I may have written gloomily on occasion, but my activities for the most part were influenced by the more cheerful, pleasure-seeking mood.

There were regular *Cherwell* lunches, and at one I found myself sitting next to Iris Murdoch. She looked like a pretty Russian peasant, but inscrutable. Searching for something to say to her that would stimulate a conversation, I foolishly asked her what made her write what she wrote. "It is an organic necessity," she said, and that was that. Most of my writing was reviews and interviews. I interviewed Nova Pilbeam in the Randolph, hoping that as many as possible of my acquaintances would see me having coffee with her, but they must all have been in other hotels or pubs that night. A glamorous, sexy actress (Lili Palmer?) was in a play at the New Theatre, but when I sent round my *Cherwell* card for an interview in her dressing-room I was told nothing doing, five or six self-styled *Cherwell* writers had tried that one on already. However, I saw Pamela Brown make her debut as Juliet at the Playhouse and gave her a rave review just before James Agate.

In The Eastgate there was a statuesque barmaid, Rita. She refused her favours to a fellow-Queensman, or, perhaps, withdrew them; I didn't know him well enough to be in his confidence. He hired a squad of men with sandwich-boards, and for a whole day they stalked through Oxford proclaiming: "Rita is unfair to David. Don't buy Rita's beer." It was the only organised 'demo' I remember, though there were some ugly scenes when politicians spoke at meetings. Noel-Baker got a very rough reception from those much further to the left then he. This same group in the Labour Club, with whom I was an ineffectual and increasingly more bored fellow-traveller, was constantly at war with the orthodox Labour Party followers, led by Tony Crosland. At the time I felt he was too smooth to be trustworthy, but looking back I think he showed both courage and consistency in defending moderate principles and policies against vigorous and unscrupulous communist attacks.

A man in Univ saw me punting, displaying bright red braces. He proposed putting me on the list of those he was going to kill, but Elliott persuaded him that there were others more deserving of an early death; and why go outside one's own college? In fact, the man was in earnest. A few days later, from his room near the porter's lodge, he shot people as they came out of lunch in Hall. He killed one and wounded one or two others. They put him away in Broadmoor.

I went to a party where the drink was Lamb's Wool. I forget whether the base was beer or wine, but it was mixed with stewed apple and cream and cinnamon, and for all I know several other ingredients, and heated in a cauldron. A Yugoslav called Mihailovitch told me it was possible to get stuck inside, and unable to withdraw from, a woman. It had happened to a pair he knew in a box at the theatre in Belgrade. They had had to be taken out on a stretcher and driven to the hospital to be uncoupled. I said I'd heard of it happening to dogs; had they perhaps been fucking in a dog-like posture? No, Mihailovitch said, he had seen the stretcher on its way to the ambulance, there was a blanket over them, of course, but they were definitely face to face, the man on top of the woman in the orthodox position. It could happen to anyone, then, I said. Well, it was very unusual, said Mihailovitch; he himself didn't know of any other case. He urged me not to let it put me off. I thanked him for his encouragement and we had some more Lamb's Wool. It acted as a soporific in the end. Instead of getting noisier and noisier, the party quietly and gradually collapsed. People slept on the floor and in chairs.

Roger Sharrock was in the Army. Elliott and I met him one vac in Leeds. His uniform didn't fit, the sleeves of his battledress reached nowhere near his wrists, and he had coal dust in his hair and round his eyes. He had been on a fatigue, he said. He was stoical but subdued. It was depressing. Elliott said Roger was the civilisation we were defending; he shouldn't have to go to war himself. Later, we heard that he'd been 'returned to unit' from his OCTU, and the rumour was that in his clumsiness he had broken a machine-gun, beyond repair. In fact, I discovered, we had heard wrongly. Roger had returned himself to his unit, entirely on his own initiative, finding that he could no longer bear the stupidity of the staff and the sycophancy of his fellow-cadets. Then he was ill, and the Army decided to release him. I wondered if his attempts at soldiering had offended the Army's aesthetic standards and he had therefore been 'excused war' as he had been 'excused games' at school. Today, when I compare my own cynical attitude and chameleon tactics in the Army with Roger's honesty, I feel quite ashamed.

I had decided that during what I thought would most probably turn out to be my one and only year at Oxford I would play different games from those on which at school I had spent so much time and energy attempting to acquire some skill. I played soccer instead of rugby, squash instead of fives, and in the hot summer of Dunkirk and the fall of France I gave up cricket and played tennis almost every afternoon. Andrew Sachnovsky was the stylist, relaxed to the point of indolence, as if he should have had one of his family's serfs to run for the difficult ones; when I met him after the War he was working for one of the big oil companies and had changed his name to something unmemorably English. Victor

Hallett hit hard. He had a rough time with the partisans in Italy. He came back in 1945 to read law, and I went to his wedding in Lincoln's Inn. Drummond Allison, the most extrovert poet I ever knew, bounced about the court like a second ball. He was killed in North Africa. The courts were down by the river, and in the early evening we would drink pints of ice-cold shandy in the pavilion before walking back to beer in the buttery. Often there was a barrel-organ at the corner of Queen's Lane. John Heath-Stubbs, almost blind, moved up the High in fits and starts from one imperfectly observed landmark to the next. Black-gowned girls cycled home from the Radcliffe Camera, twittering like starlings. The news was always bad. There didn't seem much point in trying to write elegantly on Virgil when Hitler was lurching about Europe, knocking it all down. More and more, I went over to The Eastgate after Hall.

I didn't have much to do with girls in Oxford in '39 and '40. I was having an affair with one in Huddersfield. I wrote a poem for her. It was published in *The Cherwell*, and a few years ago my daughters discovered that particular issue of the magazine in an old tin trunk. The first line was 'Let your calligraphy be physical'. It was the funniest thing they had ever read. "What does it mean? And whose 'calligraphy'?" "It means what it says. Don't you know you can't précis a poem? It was to a girl I was keen on." They thought that was even funnier. "You wait!" I told them.

As soon as Oxford was over I went walking in the Lake District with three friends who had never been up north. We ran down a steep scree, nearly falling into

Wastwater. In the pub a large, red-cheeked girl brought us bread and cheese and beer. The cheese was crawling, and we pointed this out to her. "Ee," she said, "some folks asks for maggots." We argued about the War. Freddie Gillott was a conscientious objector. He went into the Fire Service, was in London during the Blitz, and had a worse time than any of us.

Amor Interruptus

Two miles farther, the road went out on to the moors, always cold and windy, but here in the wood against the hillside all was calm and warm and green, as nearly exotic as a Yorkshire summer evening could become. We climbed the dry-stone wall and walked the few yards through the trees to take us out of sight. The grass was thick and damp. We lay on a macintosh and kissed. The flesh above her stockings was smooth and soft. In the still air I could smell her sex over the scents of earth and vegetation. The end was hurried when twigs cracked up the hill behind us and in hot fear of being discovered we lay apart and fumbled fastenings back. She put her knickers in her bag. There was no one there after all. We lit cigarettes, and their sharp fragrance dispersed the other odours of the wood and of ourselves.

Appropriately, perhaps, this was in Grimscar Wood, just above the fields where, nearly ten years before, the stranger had told Victor King and me some of the facts of life.

Sheila had a fat, slow-spoken mother, who took often

to her bed with headaches. Her father was gaunt and shaggy-browed, solemnly knowing on cricket and the price of wool-tops. Sheila was tall, tall and slim, with long brisk legs. She wore tweed skirts, and green jumpers over white shirt blouses. I don't remember her in dresses, ever. She liked Sibelius, and would lie sprawled, listening to the record of *The Swan of Tuonela* that I had given her, her bra removed from beneath her blouse so that all could be decent quickly if we heard her mother lumber out of bed. Father, a journalist, seemed hardly ever there in the evenings. They lived in a bungalow on an unmade road projecting into fields. It was only half a mile from where I lived.

My father and Sheila's both belonged to a club which met in winter for dinner and a talk by a local celebrity, preferably a sportsman, in a pub called The Pack Horse in the middle of the town. In summer they went out to a country pub which had a bowling green. That's how I met Sheila. She had a little box-like car and used to drive her father and mine to this country pub; I would go with them and she and I would return together, leaving the men to their beer and bowls. On Sunday afternoons, when I was home from school and, later, Oxford, we'd go for walks on the moors and she'd come home with me for tea. I was furious at my father. He had a running joke with her about a pair of pyjamas he was urging her to make for him; he was waiting, he said, and he said it every time Sheila came to the house, for her to tell him when the pyjamas would be ready for fitting. My mother always laughed, quickly, as soon as he had said it, not only because it was her custom to laugh whenever my father made a joke, but also, I think, on this occasion, to nip in the bud any feeling on either Sheila's part or mine that there could be anything serious behind his frivolous remark.

She was three or four years older than I, and no doubt this was part of the attraction. It meant that she had other boy friends, and this gave grounds for jealousy, which every young man's first romantic love demands. The one I feared most was Austin, a burly chap with ginger hair and freckled hands. He rode a powerful motorcycle and was a TA sergeant in the Gunners. I could see his machine parked outside her house when I walked across the fields, and this gave me the opportunity to moon into the woods, composing wistful or bitter verse, the best of which (i.e. the nearest to Auden or MacNeice) I would show her when we went to our pub across the golf course.

"Do you go to bed with Austin?"

"Yes. Sometimes."

"Would you go to bed with me? I mean, really go to bed? In a hotel? For a whole night?"

"Darling, of course. It would be lovely."

All this coming back in the dark, the wind crashing in the trees between the fairways. Instead of being elated by her quick acceptance, I thought of all that I would have to do: find an excuse to be away from home, pick a place to go, book a hotel, buy French letters. Why wasn't it enough to take her into Grimscar Woods again, where I had first dared to make love to her, or to suggest it casually now and lie down with her on the lee side of a wall in the springy grass? Too much Sibelius and César Franck, perhaps.

We settled at last for a square, stone pub, The Angel,

not far from Harrogate. My story to my parents was a visit to Haworth with Brontë-haunted friends from Oxford. To cope with my father's questions afterwards, I looked it all up in the gazetteer, the parsonage, the relics, the village. In bed at nights I practised putting Durex on; I hadn't had one with me in Grimscar Woods.

I had booked separate rooms at The Angel. I didn't think I looked old enough to play the part of a married man in front of waiters, chambermaids and other guests. We drank beer in Harrogate. When I went round to her room, she was in bed, in a pale blue nightdress. It was fun kissing her in new places, and she manipulated me without embarrassment. I was too relieved to notice at the time the disappointment in her voice when she asked me if I'd come. I think most of all I enjoyed going to sleep all mixed up with her and warm and sticky. Early in the morning I went back to my own cold bed. Vacuum cleaners hummed in the corridors. Floorboards creaked. I wondered how old I would be before I stopped minding what other people saw and thought.

When I joined the Army she was already driving ambulances. We could not see each other much, and there was a frantic air about our meetings as if a film had been speeded up and must inevitably break. Her family seemed more morose than ever. She had a plump and sexy sister who was said to be having an affair with a Roman Catholic priest, and the fear of scandal seemed to intensify her mother's hypochondria and her father's natural gloom.

In the spring of 1941 I had a week's leave. One night we went to the ballet in Leeds. We chose a slow train back because it wouldn't have a corridor and we could be private in our compartment, but although that made us safe from interruption when the train was moving, there were stops at stations every few minutes and we seemed to be for ever putting protuberant parts of our bodies back under the covering of clothes. Walking home with her, I leaned her against the sandbags outside Crowther & Sons' engineering works and kissed her slowly. Then the air raid warning wailed and I decided I'd better get her to her bungalow. I don't remember a definite 'last time'. It was probably the night we went to a dance given by the organisation for which she drove trucks and ambulances. We danced little and drank much, and someone drove us home. It wasn't much of a farewell. Then I went overseas and our relationship petered out in letters from Bangalore and Quetta. From Burma I never wrote to her at all.

I saw her once again, in 1945, when I'd been repatriated. She was married to Austin and living within a mile or two of The Angel, where we had spent our night. Austin, redder-faced and fatter, was on leave, but he was going fishing; he went off with a seething bag of bait. Sheila looked stale and soiled, and a two-year-old child whined around the house. She went upstairs to change and I didn't follow her. She strapped the child in a push-chair and we went out for a walk. It was a blazing hot July day and I was sweating; I hadn't got used to wearing thick serge battledress again. Afterwards we drank tea and she suggested putting on a record; she still had *The Swan of Tuonela*. I had to go, I had to have the truck back by six o'clock, I said. It was sad, I know, but then I just wanted to get back to the enormous Mess at Catterick and drink beer until the War ended.

You Lucky People!

When I went home from Oxford in 1940 I packed away in an old square wooden tuck-box that I'd had at school all my lecture notes and essays and those manuscripts that had never made it into print in *The Cherwell.* It was not so much that I was optimistic enough to imagine myself at Oxford again after the War, actually making use of them, but rather that I was keeping an option open. In a mood of 'you never know', it seemed to me that preservation was more fitting than destruction. In fact, when I came to look at them again, five years later, they were like fragments of pottery or mosaic, archaeological evidence of an earlier, more advanced civilization, of a much more innocent self.

There were two soldiers billeted on us in the house, from a Welsh regiment that was re-equipping and recuperating after a bad time at Dunkirk. Evans was short and dark and powerful; he looked like a prop forward from Llanelli. He was a great talker, not about the War but about the conquests he was making in the town and the pubs he took the girls to. His oppo was tall and thin and silent. They must have drunk fantastic quantities of beer, and sometimes we could hear them being sick when they came back late at night. They were skilled at vomiting, as if the technique had been drilled into them, and there was never a trace the next morning of their indisposition of a few hours earlier. My mother grew quite fond of them and cooked them large, nourishing meals.

My father was still nagging at me to go into the Navy. In view of the Admiralty's lack of eagerness to accept my services on the day war broke out, he now came up with the idea that I should qualify myself to became a Wireless Officer; he had discovered a school for this purpose in Manchester. There was a month or two to go before I needed to volunteer, or would be called up, so I thought I might as well have a bash. The school taught only the sketchiest outlines of wireless theory. It concentrated on the sending and reading of morse. We were split into groups of four or five at tables fitted with keys and headphones, and nearly all day we tapped away to one another. We were supposed to do half in code, half in what was called 'plain language', but code was considered boring and the 'plain language' proportion soon went up to about 90%. It became the custom for the one who was transmitting to insert an incongruous obscenity into a sentence every now and then, to add interest to an otherwise monotonous operation. The others in my group sent their messages from morning newspapers, usually the *Daily Express* or the *Daily Mail.* My messages were all from *War and Peace*, which I was reading at the time. It was not a popular choice, the outlandish Russian names being particularly disliked, and eventually those receiving my messages began to distort the names; when they read a passage back for checking, Prince Bolkonsky had become 'Prince Ballocky' and his estate of Bald Hills, 'Bald Pills'. When Natasha became 'Nit Crusher' I gave up and resorted to the *Manchester Guardian*.

After five or six weeks of this increasingly tedious routine, I discovered that not a single person had ever graduated from the school into the Royal Navy. They all went into the Merchant Navy or the Royal Air Force. I left immediately. However, having obtained some small proficiency at morse, I decided to volunteer for the Royal Corps of Signals. I reasoned that whatever I went into I would be required to learn skills which I would regard as useless when the War was over, and that I might as well develop the one skill of this nature that I had already begun to acquire. Also, it was going against my father's wishes, which made it the more attractive to me.

I went to the Signals Depot, for basic infantry training, in October, 1940. It was at Ossett, a scruffy little town which manufactured shoddy. The billet to which I was sent was a large, battered-looking building, once a haulage company's garage. The first thing each recruit had to do was to take a long sack from a pile in the yard and stuff it with straw; this was then his palliasse, 'in lieu of', to use one of the Army's favourite terms, mattress. A bed was three planks on two low trestles. There were four long lines of these. Buckets were placed here and there to catch rain when it fell from the larger leaks in the roof. Smaller leaks, even if directly above a bed, were ignored, and the NCO i/c Billet had the absolute right to decide whether a leak qualified for a bucket. Whatever his decision, beds could only be moved sideways to avoid leaks, never forwards or backwards; the alignment of a row of beds was sacrosanct. One wall had windows, and the unfortunates in the row of beds beneath them had the task of fitting heavy blackout screens in place at dusk and removing them at dawn—or 'sparrow fart', as the Army charmingly described the day's beginning. There was a room across the yard known as 'the ablutions'. This had no windows and only one, extremely weak, electric light bulb; shaving in this perpetual twilight, and in cold water, too, was not easy, and most of us bought candles to supplement the inadequate illumination. Behind the ablutions were the latrines, a row of three-walled cubicles, the walls made of sacking tacked to wooden posts. In each cubicle a roughly carpentered wooden seat was placed over a trench. There were no doors, of course. Lavish use was made of an exceptionally strong disinfectant, so strong that it brought tears to your eyes as you sat there, but still not strong enough entirely to overcome the smell of shit.

We were issued with uniform and equipment, including leather bandoliers, and rifles. The bandolier, a series of leather pouches on a leather strap, had to be in a high state of polish all the time. When you weren't wearing it on parade, it had to be laid out in a certain position on your bed, with the rest of your kit, gleaming for inspection. The Lance-Corporal in charge of our squad told us about boots. An Army Order had just been published to the effect that all boots would henceforth be dubbined. There was to be an end to the practice of 'burning and boning'. "But," said Lance-Corporal Hardy, "it so happens that there is no way known to man nor beast of acquiring a properly shining toecap without the aforesaid burning and boning—and that, as I have already informed yew, is forbidden. Strict-lee for-bidden. I will now demonstrate to yew this strictly forbidden method of getting the right degree of polish on the toecaps of your boots. The only degree of polish which will enable yew to be properly dressed when on parade." He showed us how to burn and bone. "Now," he glared at us as he reached his peroration, "if I catches—catches, mark yew, see what I mean—anybody burning and boning, that man willl be on a charge so quick his feet won't touch the ground. So just don't let me catch anyone, see what I mean?" We got the message. Soon the latrines were full of men burning and boning their boots, while a sentry stood at one end of the line of cubicles to warn of the approach of Lance-Corporal Hardy or any other NCO or officer.

We queued to tell an officer our religion and have it entered in our documents. There was much argument in the queue about the best thing to say. "Tell him you're a fucking Buddhist," argued one man. "That'll fox 'em. They won't have Buddhist Church Parades laid on, will they?" Opinion, in the end, came down against him. "If you says you're a bleeding Buddhist or an atheist or something they'll have you on fucking fatigues Sunday mornings. Church Parade's a piece of cake. Once you're there you can have a good kip. You put down C of E, mate. That's favourite." This seemed sensible advice, and most of us took it. It was based on the sound principle of never doing anything to draw attention to yourself.

There were exceptions to that rule, of course. One man in the squad was a music-hall contortionist in 'civvy street'. He was determined to get his cards. He said that he could control his bowels and go without a shit for weeks. That would shake 'em. Chronic constipation. They'd have to get rid of him. He reported sick and was admitted to a nearby military hospital. Rumours reached us. He had gone four days without. Ten days. Three weeks. We never saw him again, and by the time our six weeks' basic training was completed it was said that he had actually been discharged.

Foot drill, rifle drill and bullshit were the three main occupations. "Bags of swank! Bags of swank!" shrieked Lance-Corporal Hardy as we marched up the road towards the Guard on the main gate. One afternoon he made us throw our rifles at one another and learn to catch them coming at us, hard, from any angle. This, he explained, was because we had to treat the rifle as an extension of the body, like an extra arm or leg. I couldn't follow his reasoning. I couldn't think of any occasion when your own leg would be thrown at you, unless you were at death's door. However, I quite enjoyed the exercise. It was the nearest to cricket that we ever got.

We were taught the slow march indoors, in a big hall where there was a piano. On this Lance-Corporal Hardy played an eccentric version of 'Over the sea to Skye', at the same time making a throaty, whining noise as if in imitation of bagpipes. It was the only endearing thing he ever did. To this accompaniment we tottered like zombies from one end of the hall to the other.

The worst time of all was being woken up in the morning. "Rise and shine! You lucky people! Take your hands off it!"—the dawn chorus of strutting, stamping, shouting NCOs. The struggle to find a tap and shave in the half light. Then there was a march of just over a mile to the mess hall for tea and bacon and fried bread, with Daddy's Sauce. Once that was over, the day seemed tolerable, though unnaturally long. "Right, break off for three minutes for a spit and a drag!" meant, in Lance-Corporal Hardy's squad, exactly three minutes, not a moment more. I took to Woodbines and kept dog-ends. However fiercely you drew at a cigarette you couldn't smoke one right through in three minutes. I was perpetually hungry. If there was time after lunch, I rushed into the canteen for a quick pie and beans. At night I hungered for egg and chips more than I thirsted for pints of bitter.

After the passing-out parade some squads took their instructor out for a drink. We decided not to waste good beer on Lance-Fucking-Corporal Bloody Kiss-Me-Hardy, to give him his full name. He had a mouth like a piece of wire. He yelled abuse as if he meant it, not as if it were the stylised language of a play, which was the way most instructors treated it. He was sarcastic. He was cocky. Nobody minded "I'll have your guts for garters!" being bawled at them, but Hardy personalized his taunts, applying them to a man's job or background. Oxford undergraduates—there were two of us in the squad—were supposed by him to be afraid of getting their feet wet; he delighted in sending us stamping to a halt in the deepest puddle he could find, knowing it meant extra work on boots, gaiters and trousers later.

At the end of November we were posted to Training Battalions to 'learn a trade'. The Army slipped up in my case and posted me to the Battalion in my home town when they could have sent me to North Wales. I was billeted in an old roller-skating rink. The place couldn't have been colder if it had been an ice-skating establishment. The despised 'pants, long, woollen' were worn at night with pyjamas and pullovers to try to keep from freezing. A onetime booking-clerk from Goole Station fell drunk on his bed one night and set fire to his palliasse with his cigarette. He was snoring happily, his bedding and kitbag glowing red, when the smoke roused the rest of us at midnight. He had so much pay docked for the damage done to his kit and uniform that we had to pay for his beer for months.

I was learning to be a Wireless Operator. Being able already to send and read morse, however slowly, I was put in what was called 'the Advanced Squad'. Everyone else in it had been a telegraphist in the Post Office. They were in a different league. It was as if they had developed an extra sense, just for morse. They could read a book while receiving a message in code at over thirty words a minute.

A corporal, a local man, was killed in an air-raid on London. His body was brought back to be buried in a churchyard in his village up the Colne Valley. Six of us from the Advanced Squad were detailed as coffin-bearers. We met, with the sergeant in charge, at the undertaker's headquarters, a pub in Fartown near the Rugby League ground. We waited for hours, drinking pints and pints of beer, before the proceedings started. When we got to the churchyard we were drunk. It was a steep hill-side, with patches of frozen snow. We were the most ill-assorted set of coffin-bearers they could have found. The tallest of us was about six foot six, the shortest not much over five foot, and the rest of us were all of varying heights between these extremes. The sergeant, who must have been pretty drunk himself, neglected to sort us out so that the tallest of us would be on the lower side of the sloping path. The parson and a group of mourning relatives watched as we stumbled up the path, swaying, hiccupping, stopping every now and then to shift the weight and keep the coffin from falling to the iron-hard ground. "Steady, lads!" said the sergeant, soothingly. By the time the service was over the pubs were shut for the afternoon, but the sergeant knew the landlord of a pub on the road back, and we were admitted to the kitchen. We sat there by a big fire, drinking more pints of bitter, and the sergeant told rambling, pointless stories about the North West Frontier.

As a 'potential officer' I was summoned before several selection boards. Someone always asked: "What characteristics do you think a good officer should have?" There were stock answers to this. One was Initiative, another was Sense of Humour. It was like knowing your catechism. An ancient-looking colonel once remarked: "I see that when you went up to Oxford you changed from the oval to the round ball." I lied glibly, showing Initiative, I suppose. "Yes, sir. I thought I'd meet more soccer- than rugger-players in the ranks when I joined the Army." There were nods all round, and approving grunts. A few days later I was made an Acting Unpaid Lance-Corporal, and my C.O. told me I was booked for OCTU in a month or two.

I had a friend called Shelton who'd been in the next bed to mine at the Depot. He was a London University graduate and a card-carrying communist. After appearing before the first selection board he was not summoned to any more. No reason was given, and Shelton was sure they had found out he was a communist. He didn't seem to mind. His girl friend had followed him up north and had taken a job on the local buses. Also, she had acquired a caravan to live in, and Shelton spent most of his free time there. She was a stringy redhead, with not much conversation, but she was "a good bunk-up", Shelton told me. He was accustomed to regular sex and said he could tell, from the effect on him, that the stories about a sexual depressant being put in the soldiers' porridge from time to time were absolutely true. You could counteract it, though, he said, with Guinness.

It was a hard winter, and they had us out hacking away with pick-axes at the blocks of ice that covered the main roads to Leeds and Bradford. After a week or two of this, a corporal came round and asked if any of us who were booked for OCTU wanted to do our training in India. I thought about India for a moment. A land free from snow and ice and slush. Dark girls with globular breasts. Bananas, mangoes, curries. Yes, Corporal, I said, I did. The corporal, an old sweat, had been to India. He urged me to think again. I felt as if I'd got frost-bite in my fingers and I told him I couldn't think of any place I wanted to go to more than India. He put me on the list, though he obviously thought I was round the bend. "You wait till you see all those wogs," he said. "India's full of fucking wogs!"

Nothing happened about this for months, and everybody said serve you bloody right, never volunteer for anything, you'll be posted to John o'fucking Groats. Then, suddenly, I was given a week's embarkation leave and told to report to Aldershot in a draft for India. At Aldershot we were not yet in an OCTU, but we had become cadets, so everybody had to keep his old badge of rank and wear a white band round his cap as well. 'We' were sergeant-majors, quartermaster-sergeants, bombardiers, troopers, sappers, signalmen, privates, now all cadets as well. We had proper bunks at last, and for mattresses three square objects like hard cushions, known as 'biscuits'.

Aldershot in May had a bizarre prettiness, the chestnut trees in flower against the grim old cavalry barracks, the streets of the garrison town transformed to leafy boulevards, as if Proust were re-writing Kipling. The days were spent square-bashing and route-marching, having inoculations, blood groupings and medical inspections, and discussing rumours of our sailing date. In the evenings there was nothing to do but drink. We avoided the pubs frequented by the Toronto Scottish. A few weeks before we arrived, they had whooped it up in Aldershot, picking fights, insulting women and

C*

breaking windows. They had been read the riot act and were now much chastened; in the evenings they could be seen practising baseball on the square outside their barracks. However, it was said that the slightest thing might set them off again, and that one of the things that irritated them was the sight of a cadet's white-ribboned cap in any pub where they were drinking. Unexpectedly, the first time I encountered them, it was to team up, two Canadians and two of us, to go in search of women. Where we found the camp-followers, I cannot now remember, but their only pleasant attribute seemed to be their extreme willingness to please. We ended up, after the pubs had shut, in a small, stuffy terrace house. The women had dirty underwear, and as there were only two of them, we were able to leave them to the exclusive attentions of the wild colonial boys.

I became friendly, for no reason that I can now imagine, with a man called Tom Berry. He was square-jawed, pipe-smoking, and actually liked being in the Army. He behaved as if he had round his neck a placard saying 'I am Good Officer Material'. He talked of horses and pheasants and trout. He regarded the War as a specially exciting kind of blood-sport. When we were given a final 48-hour leave and forbidden to go more than fifty miles away, he invited me home with him. He lived in a charming little seventeenth century house on the edge of the Cotswolds. He had got married only a few months earlier and confided to me in the train that he was disappointed that his wife was not yet pregnant. "I must do something about that this weekend," he said; he clenched his teeth round his pipe and stared out of the window with grim determination, as if contemplating a last-ditch attack upon the hitherto impregnable defences of his wife. I pictured her as a big-boned, hearty countrywoman who would make a splendid Colonel's Lady in years to come. She turned out to be nothing like that at all. She was tiny, very pretty, with a creamy skin and thick, glossy, dark hair, shy but welcoming; she had read books that Tom had never heard of and would have considered subversive if he had. I felt sorry for her, protective. What could they have in common? She deserved a romantic lover, not an insensitive husband bent only on insemination.

I was put in the room next to theirs. All night, it seemed, there were rattles and squeaks, exclamations, moans and mutterings. My heart bled for her. She was so fragile. She would break, surely. In the morning, subdued, bruised, she would signal me for help. Not a bit of it. She looked marvellous. Talk about the lineaments of gratified desire! Tom was smug. "If that hasn't done the trick I'm a Dutchman," he said as we walked down to his local for a beer before lunch. It had, too. Three or four months later, in Bangalore, he sought me out to tell me the good news, and we got drunk on Indian whisky. After all, I had listened in to the conception.

At last, early one morning, we marched in a long column to the station. At the head of the column was the pipe band of the Toronto Scottish. They may have been a help to 'A' Company, but to us in 'C' Company, several hundreds of yards and three or four bends in the road behind, they were a pain in the neck. We marched through changes of step as if through a rough sea.

We were in the train for nearly twenty-four hours. The stations were all called Virol or Bovril or Mazzawattee Tea, but we went through Oxford, because I recognised the gasworks. In the middle of the night someone identified Berwick-on-Tweed. Just before dawn we ended up on Clydeside. We stood on the wharf and were given mugs of tea. As it grew less dark we could see a battleship, a cruiser, two or three destroyers and a mixed bag of passenger liners and cargo ships. We were taken off by lighter to our ship. It was a Canadian Pacific liner called 'The Empress of Japan'.

There were two very drunk members of 'The Empress of Japan's' crew on the lighter. They exhorted us to look at the ship's bows and bridge as we approached. There were lots of holes of differing shapes and sizes, some neat and round as if they had been made deliberately by the ship's engineer, perhaps for reasons of ventilation, others long and jagged, as though some madman had been let loose with a pick-axe. "A present from Jerry," said one of the sailors. "I wonder what he's been saving up for us this time?" The ship loomed, grey, battered, menacing, as we drew alongside. The sailors sang 'Glasgae belongs tae me' in Liverpool accents, and one of them threw an empty half-bottle of whisky into the water.

From Greenland's Icy Mountains

In the train I had sat next to a man called McKinley and after the twenty-hour journey we were friends. Most Army friendships begin not from choice but from propinquity, such as having adjacent bed spaces or sharing certain duties. It doesn't make them any less valuable. They have some of the advantages of arranged marriages over more romantic relationships. You don't start by being blind to the other's differences and defects, and you build on a strong base of tolerance.

McKinley had in fact been a corporal instructor at Ossett. I'd never spoken to him there but I'd often thought I'd rather have been in his squad than in Lance-Corporal Hardy's. He was full of bounce but not bumptious. He liked being good at things, and his saving grace was that he could laugh at the things in which he had made himself proficient; his drill was perfect, but it had the flamboyant brilliance of the actor who doesn't quite believe in the play in which he stars. Drunk one night, he stood stark naked on a table and recited 'The Green Eye of the Little Yellow God' in a broad Scots accent. Before the War he had worked in a men's outfitters in Glasgow.

As soon as we got on board 'The Empress of Japan' McKinley disappeared. He came back to tell me that he had put us both down for the anti-submarine watch. When I protested about never volunteering he told me to wait till I'd had a look below. "It'll be like the bloody Black Hole of Calcutta in a day or two." He was right. The port-holes were permanently shut. Sleeping was either in a hammock or on a mattress on the floor underneath. When the hammocks were slung and men were in them they formed a solid mass; if you came late to your own it was almost impossible to prise the rest apart so that you could mount. Underneath there wasn't even the width of a boot between one mattress and the next. On the first night the atmosphere grew foetid. What it would be like in the tropics didn't bear thinking of. In the morning hammocks and mattresses had to be stowed away and kit laid out for ship's inspection. It was made clear at the first of these that standards would be high; greatcoat buttons and cap badges had to be polished to perfection. We were issued with life jackets and told that we had to have them with us at all times. On parades we would wear them, the rest of our waking time we would carry them, at night we would use them as pillows. Anyone found without his life jacket, it didn't matter what he was doing, even shaving or shitting, was for the high jump. There were rumours that as we were ultimately under naval discipline men could be 'put in irons' and banished to some fearful nether region of the ship. A klaxon sounded and we had our first lifeboat drill. It was a shambles, we were told, and too slow by half. There would be lifeboat drills at any hour of the day or night from now on until we pulled our fingers out.

We stayed immobile in the Clyde off Greenock for three days. Then, one evening, we moved off. The hills, with the slanting sun on them, were green and gold and mauve. I had never been to Scotland before, but McKinley said we would actually sail past his home town of Rothesay on the Isle of Bute. He stood at the rail, getting more and more excited, jumping up and down and pointing. As the sun set, the estuary opened out and there was sea all round us, moving; we began to learn how to walk differently, to avoid staggering. We were next in line behind the battleship. The other ships spread out, and the destroyers rushed backwards and forwards on the flanks. We seemed to be going very slowly and a knowledgeable person said we could only go as fast as the slowest ship in the convoy and anyway, what were we binding about, the fucking cruise was free, wasn't it? Another knowledgeable person said we were steaming north of west, which wasn't exactly the shortest way to India but was to get out of range of German aircraft, bloody quick, because if any aircraft saw us he'd whistle up the U-boats, and then kybosh, sitting fucking ducks we were at this speed. Cras ingens iterabimus aequor, I said, but only to myself.

McKinley and I and several other pairs were on a two-hours-on, eight-hours-off lookout. The weather got colder and windier every day. Two or three small land-birds appeared and perched on the rails, and yet another knowledgeable person said we were just off Greenland. There had been one nasty moment when a plane, presumably German on reconnaissance, was spotted on the starboard side of the convoy, and a cruiser, its anti-aircraft guns sounding like a guard-dog's barking, chased it off. The convoy zigzagged like mad and everyone said wait for it, the U-boats were on their way. We watched and watched for any streak of phosphorescence that might betray a periscope, but nothing happened.

If we came off watch at night we went down to the galley for mugs of cocoa. The ship creaked rhythmically. One night a cadet dropped his mug and fell down in an epileptic fit. Somebody put a spoon in his mouth to stop him biting his tongue off. It was said that this would end his career as a cadet, if not as a soldier, and that as soon as we got to Bombay he'd be put on the first boat back.

'B' Deck was unbelievably sordid when you came off watch. A lot of men were seasick and queuing to get into the lavatories. As they queued they vomited. It was the nearest I came to being sick, seeing them in this state. McKinley had a word with the officer in charge of our look-out and he let us take our mattresses and sleep on the mess tables. This got us out of the worst of the overcrowding, and the smell of old food was preferable to that of fresh vomit, but we could have done without the cockroaches that woke us up as they crawled across our faces.

The battleship left us and returned to the Clyde to escort other convoys into the mid-Atlantic. We turned south and the weather got warmer. We put on tropical kit for the first time. Off Freetown we anchored but were not allowed on shore. Bumboats swarmed, and nearly naked men implored us to throw them "Glasgow tanners, Tommy, Glasgow tanners!" They dived to catch the coins, only rarely failing to intercept them before they hit the harbour bottom. With the ship motionless, the heat grew almost unbearable. 'B' Deck was bad enough; what could it be like on 'C', 'D' and 'E' Decks? Would India be as hot? It didn't seem possible. Before we left Freetown I was put on the fizzer for not having my greatcoat buttons adequately polished on ship's inspection. I had to spend a couple of hours in a hold lifting out crates of beer for the officers' mess. Each defaulter was given a bottle at the end of the fatigue, and most of us managed to snitch another as well. Our canteen was 'dry' and this was the first beer I'd had since sailing. It was good, but not worth the sweat that had earned it.

In Cape Town we were allowed shore leave. People were waiting at the dock gates to invite us out to tea and a drive round Table Mountain. A Jewish couple took McKinley and me and we picnicked in a vineyard behind the mountain; at last we were out of sight of that bloody sea we'd been on for four weeks. In the evening Mac and I went round the bars. It was my twenty-first birthday. The party grew, and finished up in a place called the Del Monico, in Adderley Street, which had a ceiling painted like the night-sky. We were drunk, of course, when we got back to the ship, but not so drunk, we learned the next morning, as eight unfortunates who hadn't even seen the gangplank and had fallen into the harbour and been drowned. When we put to sea again we discovered there'd been several desertions, too, but nothing to equal the last convoy. From that, God knows how many men had deserted, some stories said thirty, some three hundred, and commandeered a train and driven off towards the veldt; all the stories agreed that they had not been seen since, and there was envious speculation that they might be able to live undetected in the bush until the end of the War.

The anti-submarine look-out had been too good to last. Now I was on a watertight door watch instead. This was a great come-down. You sat, by yourself, on a camp stool somewhere down near the bottom of the ship. There was nothing to do unless the instruction came to close the watertight door. It was so boring that there were three cases of cadets falling asleep while on watch. They were court-martialled, to be returned to unit from Bombay. The particular watertight door I 'watched' was by a hold in which the meat was stored. After I'd seen the lascars climbing over the meat in their bare feet and hawking and spitting on it, the food never tasted quite the same again. It had been getting worse anyway. Nearly every meal ended with a gooey sago or tapioca pudding, and some wag suggested that the cooks tossed each other off all day to produce this unappetising substance.

The final stage of the seven-week voyage was in a way the worst. The tension was off, nobody expected U-boats or enemy aircraft now, and boredom was acute. Curiously, the one occupation more and more grew keen on was housey-housey, which I would have thought was boredom organized to the nth degree. Sometimes I listened, fascinated, to the cry of "Eyes down, looking!" as hundreds of men prepared to be mesmerised for an hour or two each night. We were all temporarily insulated from the War and its dangers and objectives, the ship was a squalid, floating slum, the sea flat and featureless, the air, even on deck, thick and hot and humid, and perhaps it was appropriate that a roomful of grown men could sit bowed like a congregation before their priest as he intoned the magic abracadabra, "legs eleven", "clickety-click" and "un-luck-ee thirteen".

In the last few days we ceased even to speculate about India and our future there. We didn't care what India was like. It could have been full of scorpions and rabid dogs and we would still have welcomed it. We just wanted an end to troopship life. Roll on, Bombay!

To India's Coral Strand

In Aldershot they had issued us with sun helmets of a design worn by nineteenth century explorers in Africa. When we got to Bombay we handed them in and were given in exchange more functional, less romantic-looking headgear. Presumably the old helmets went back and forth across the Indian and Atlantic Oceans for the rest of the War. It seemed a suitably daft introduction to Army life in India.

The troop train to Bangalore was not so hot as the ship, but there was a new menace. In the Deccan the fields appeared to be composed of a highly volatile dust instead of solid earth, and the engine contributed an oily grey grit which combined with the dust to form a sticky paste on skin and clothes. We arrived, after about thirty hours, in time for a bath and breakfast. We had been given to read in the train a leaflet of Dos and Don'ts for British troops in India, and the number of forbidden activities had been depressingly large; the eating and drinking of almost anything, if it were sold to you by an

Indian outside an Army camp or cantonment, would lead to sore throats, typhoid, dysentery, and countless other incapacitating illnesses, and if you weren't attacked internally, the anopheles mosquito would get you by biting any unprotected portion of your skin. We perked up when we were shown into the Mess at Bangalore. There were bowls of fruit on the table, including bananas and mangoes; mangoes were an entirely new experience and bananas had disappeared from wartime England. Bearers flocked to serve us with our choice of tea or coffee—a choice, for Christ's sake! Oh, Lance-Corporal Hardy, you should see us now! Up yours, mate!—and great platefuls of eggs and bacon; they wore white tunics and pyjama-like trousers, turbans, and brightly striped cummerbunds. At dinner that first evening an officer stood up and said "Mr. Vice, the King Emperor!" I wondered who Mr. Vice was and how he had acquired that reputation.

In the Officers' Training School the rank was 'Gentleman Cadet', but when they saw some of our draft had been NCOs and Warrant Officers in the Regular Army the word 'Gentleman' was dropped. One of the ex-sergeants was known as 'Tank Corps Joe'. He was a great line-shooter. He had been everywhere, done everything. He was small and fiery, with piggy eyes and a bristling moustache. When I was drawn against him in a boxing tournament I lived in fear for a week. I kept going to look at the list to see if a miracle had saved me and the pairing had been changed. I hated boxing and was no good at it. The general opinion was that Tank Corps Joe would slaughter me. What kind of flowers would

I like, my friends asked me, and did I want them to write to my next of kin? In desperation I tried a succession of straight lefts. They all connected. Tank Corps Joe had even less idea of boxing than I had, and his arms were inches shorter. I gave him a black eye and a bleeding nose. In the evening people came from other companies to see who had done this to Tank Corps Joe. It was my one moment of glory at the OTS.

We went from parades to other parades or lectures on bicycles. Bicycle drill included how to ride to attention when we passed an officer, and on the command "Pile Bicycles!" how to lean one bicycle against another so that both stood up. Late in the course we did a series of day and night manoeuvres on Agram Plain, a waste-land of red, sandy earth scarred by water-courses which were either torrents for the few hours after a storm or bone-dry if there had been no rain in the preceding twelve hours. As we marched there we sang an adaptation of what I believe is an Engineers' song: "Oh we're marching on to Agram Plain, to Agram Plain, to Agram Plain, oh we're marching on to Agram Plain, where they don't know sugar from shit!"

Off duty, I liked to take a bike and explore the country-side and villages. The roads, on which the main traffic was bullock carts and buses, the latter old and frail and hugely over-loaded but driven fast and furiously, were lined by feather-duster palms; the villages were usually set back from the road in the paddy fields, and between the houses, most of them little more than huts, roamed stately water-buffaloes, scrawny, scavenging pi-dogs and energetic monkeys. There was a sprinkling of Indians among the cadets, and I was friendly with one or two, but they all came from the north and were about as far from home as a Londoner would have been in the Balkans, so I had no introduction to Indian families in the neighbourhood. The first time I had a 'night out' in the bazaar I drank too much Indian whisky and was found unconscious at midnight in a storm-conduit outside our row of bungalows. I wondered how I'd got as near to base as that, until a few days later a taxi-driver called to see me with a scrap of paper on which I had almost illegibly written that I owed the driver the sum of twelve rupees. There was said to be a brothel a few miles away staffed entirely by, of all people, White Russians, but I never met anyone who had actually been there or knew precisely where it was. Three cadets got very drunk one night and insisted that their taxi-driver take them there. They refused to believe his ignorance of its whereabouts, and shouted and swore at him until in revenge he drove them to the Commandant's house. That exalted personage had been holding a dinner-party, and his guests were not a little startled when the three drunks entered, shouted "Bring on the dancing girls!" and worse, and proceeded to goose some eminently respectable memsahibs. The last laugh, of course, was the Commandant's; all three cadets were RTUed.

After the three months' infantry course in Bangalore, those of us destined for the Signals moved for five months' specialised training in Mhow in Central India. Mhow had a cinema where you could buy curry puffs and lime juice in the bar. During the interval they played a record of a woman singing: "Oh, do it again, I just say Oh Oh Oh Oh Oh Oh do it again, you won't regret it, come and get it, Oh, do it again." Sex-starved men moaned and stamped and banged their seats.

We were taught to drive on buses that had had their commercial day. When an Indian bus has outlived its usefulness on the roads, it really is decrepit. Disconcerting things happened, like the gear lever coming away in your hand at a critical moment. However, in my time the only person who failed the final driving-test was a sad-faced man from Slough who ran over, and killed, a goat at the entrance to the bazaar.

My room-mate was Gareth Johns, a historian from Trinity College, Cambridge. Neither of us took easily to wireless theory, but Johns was good at inventing mnemonics so that we could pass our tests with quite high marks. During our course the Japs attacked Pearl Harbour and then Singapore and Burma. Johns forecast a short and brutish life for us all in the jungle. He was fond of signs and portents, and reminded me that we had come out to India on a ship called 'The Empress of Japan'.

I had a feckless friend called Pettifer. During the more boring exercises we competed in recalling idiotic verses from popular songs. I forget which of us remembered it, but by mutual consent the winning verse was:

"Oh, robins and roses,
And maybe a tree,
A poem by Kipling
While life goes rippling
By."

There was an outbreak of conjunctivitis or 'pink eye'. Pettifer and I were annoyed that as more and more cadets were removed to hospital for what we thought of as a rest, we were not catching it. We rubbed our eyes until they were sore and then reported sick. The M.O. sent us to hospital and we took in a gramophone, loads of records, books, and a bottle of gin. The nurses thought it was fun for the first day and then got fed up with us. The patients already there said whatever else you came in with you got malaria before you left. The mosquito nets were lifted at dawn, when the mozzies were at their hungriest, to suit the shift system of the hospital staff. Alarmed, we made a quick recovery and escaped without infection.

Our commissions started at 0001 hours. Or was it 2359? Anyway, one of those magic times with which the Army, in superstitious mood, bracketed the midnight hour without having to acknowledge its existence. We went to the cinema with our pips in our pockets. The film was 'Sun Valley Serenade', in which Glenn Miller and his band played 'Chattanooga Choo Choo'. When we got on the night train to go on leave we put our pips up. In the Taj Mahal Hotel in Bombay every room had a bearer allocated to its occupants; he lived in the corridor, cleaning shoes and sewing on buttons and bundling up clothes to be taken to the dhobi. People slept in the streets at night, wrapped in white cotton, like corpses. The Harbour Bar was full of Royal Navy officers with debby girls. The debbiest took McKinley and me sailing, and afterwards we drank tankards of Pimms in the Yacht Club. However, we both got the impression that she thought she had been doing her good deed for the day; it was not going to lead to anything. In Grant Road the brothels were cages, the women ugly, the price a few annas. There were higher-class establishments where you could sit and drink beer and some of the girls said they came from Egypt. This was supposed to be an advantage, Egypt being several thousand miles nearer England, but the girls struck me as being disagreeably fat and podgy; they looked as if they had been injected with butter like chickens à la Kiev.

I was posted to a unit in Quetta. We lived in what were called Wana Huts; they had tent roofs and mud walls to keep out tribesmen's bullets. It was a training unit for Indian recruits, most of whom seemed to have been press-ganged in the villages of South India. A little shrivelled nut of a man with the grand name of Babu Sahib arrived speaking no known language. Indian NCOs from units all over Baluchistan were brought to try and communicate with him in Tamil, Telegu, Malayalam and the many dialect variations on these South Indian languages. He understood nothing, spoke nothing intelligible except his own name, and eventually was sent back to his village or what was recorded as his village; even that he was unable to confirm. Other recruits saw snow for the first time and fainted on parade. The cinemas here served hot punch in the interval and you kept your greatcoat on during the performance. The swells from the Staff College wore sheepskins.

The Captain Quartermaster had been in the Army since before the '14–'18 War. In his cups one night, he confessed that he had hoped for a better posting than Quetta from his Freemason friends in GHQ India. Other

QMs, with only half his service in, "hardly got their knees brown, some of 'em", had been posted through the Freemasons' "old boy net" to Delhi, Poona, even "dear old Cal". "I can see the buggers now," he reflected enviously, "up and down Chowringhee every night, Firpo's, Grand Hotel, Great Eastern. And here am I, stuck in fucking Quetta. Worse than bloody Basra. You know what they say about Basra, don't you?" I didn't, then. "The Persian Gulf is the arsehole of the world, and Basra is five hundred miles up it." I was interested in the revelations of the Freemasonry network. My father, who, to give him credit, had said he'd never join, himself, because he couldn't have stood the mumbo-jumbo, had urged me to think seriously about becoming one. "They always stand by their own, son," he had said. For once, he had seemed not put out when I refused his proposal. When my grandfather, the one who'd run away with the barmaid, had died, all that he'd left my father, his only son, had been his Masonic regalia. I remembered the box coming, a heavy, highly-polished receptacle of walnut? mahogany? in which were various insignia, an apron and a silver trowel. My father had examined them scornfully and then banished the box to a cupboard full of old bound copies of the Illustrated London News. Perhaps, I thought, the Oedipus-Laius relationship was particularly strong in our family.

After the bitter winter, with its snows and piercing winds from Afghanistan, there was a short spring and then a long, blazing hot summer. The favourite hangover drink was no longer tea with rum in it, but 'rock shandy', a mixture of ice-cold fizzy lemonade and soda water.

The old hands said that now was the time to find your bit of crumpet; women couldn't have enough of it in the hot weather. There were a lot of married women in Quetta whose Indian Army husbands were away in North Africa in the desert, or, now, in the Burmese jungle. Army documents referred to these women as 'abandoned wives' and they were rumoured to live up to this description. I got no further than dancing with them at the Club; the Staff College competition was too fierce.

I went on a map-making expedition into Persian Baluchistan. It was thought that the Germans might defeat the Russians and attempt to invade India by this route. The area had not been mapped for fifty years. We set off in 3-ton lorries and 15-cwt trucks, not the most suitable vehicles for country where there were hardly any roads, but we had to take tents and large amounts of tinned and dried foods, and anyway, though there may have been jeeps in other parts of India by then (August, 1942), we had not yet received any in Quetta. The first snag we found was that out of the twenty or so R.I.A.S.C. drivers allotted to us only about one third had been trained long enough or well enough to be trusted to drive the heavy lorries on rough tracks on mountain sides and over river beds. This meant that on the more hair-raising stretches of the journey, where a missed gear could mean the loss of men and vehicle, the six officers had to ferry the twelve lorries and trucks to comparatively safer ground.

A regular Indian Army cavalry officer was in command. He read Gibbon's 'Decline and Fall' in the evenings when we camped. He was to report on 'tankability'. The other officers were from the Gunners, the Engineers, the Service Corps, the Medical Corps and the Signals, each of us to recce and report on his speciality. I had to find out where telegraph poles still stood and what would be needed to make them work; also to test wireless reception over the hills back to Quetta.

After a particularly dangerous drive on a precipitous track only inches wider than the lorries, the Engineer officer developed nervous paralysis and had to be sent back. The next night I had malaria and they told me in the morning that I'd stood over the M.O., pointed a shaking pistol at him and threatened to shoot him if he had any ideas about sending me back too. They fed me on eggs and whisky, and after a day or two we pushed on. It was the country that had finished off Alexander the Great's army, and you could see why. There was hardly any water and little grey thorn bushes were the only vegetation. In the villages, which were few and far between, the shops contained only a sack or two of dusty grain and some bottles of vinegar. The only animals we saw were goats. Indian villages could be squalid, but they teemed with life. Here, on the eastern edge of Persia, was poverty such as I had never seen before. All was stony, jagged, parched, and the few people who existed there looked exhausted, desiccated. Occasionally, we came upon a patch of land with water, where palms and pomegranates grew; the fresh dates were firm and juicy as apples, the pomegranates thirst-quenching beyond belief, like fountains in your mouth. We went through one valley where the temperature was said—

by the map-maker of fifty years ago—never to drop below 100°F., night or day, through the twelve months of the year. The valley opened out into a vast, dead-flat arena, ringed in the distance by hills that looked like slag heaps. For the first time we could accelerate to the limit of the lorries' speed—until I had to stamp on the brake and swerve to avoid going straight into a lake. It was an honest-to-goodness mirage. There was no water anywhere near. The 'slag heaps' when we got there were made of lava from a volcano rearing up behind. It puffed slowly, as if contemplating but not minding about the desolation it had caused. I have no diary for that time, but I think the volcano was called Koi-i-Taftun.

After a month we came to the coast, and the villages and people seemed not quite so poor. At least they had fish. Among the inhabitants were several with frizzy hair and broad nostrils, relics of the slave trade, I suppose. We turned back towards India, by a different route. We had been out of communication with Quetta for the past two weeks. We were halfway through our rations. There was a derelict telegraph line across our path. I thought I should explore it, but it was obvious that no truck could follow it where it wound into the hills. In the next village there was a camel, with its driver; they belonged to some Khan's private army. The driver understood a bit of Urdu and agreed to take me. I sat behind him on the big double saddle. We swayed and lurched up a steep hillside, the camel stumbling from time to time. It was extremely hot. I could smell burning. Could the camel be on fire? It had seemed hot-tempered when I mounted and had bubbled like a cauldron.

I traced the smell to the dangling end of the driver's turban, to which I had set fire with my cigarette. I thought the driver might be annoyed if he found out, so I spat on my hands and delicately put out the fire. The turban's owner gave no sign of noticing. After a few hours the telegraph poles petered out, so we turned back. I joined the rest of the party in the late afternoon. When I got off the camel I was bow-legged and stiff. I gave the driver rather more than the sum he had asked; there was quite a large hole in his head-cloth.

We encountered a Persian District Officer and he gave a party for us. Conversation was in a mixture of Urdu and French. The party began at six in the evening with sponge cake and beer and progressed through many savoury courses until at midnight we were drinking arak and eating a roast sheep. We had seen no live sheep in the vicinity, and the village and surrounding country looked just as dry and barren as everywhere else. I had been hardly able to eat anything for a week or two after my malaria, but now I had a convalescent's insatiable appetite; to me the seven-hour feast was a dream come true. As we ate, an old man played a fiddle, more and more hysterically and acrobatically, the instrument held now above his head, now behind his back, faster and faster, while a small boy danced lasciviously, vibrating like a tuning fork. The District Officer said the old man was famous and had played on Teheran Radio.

A day or two later we went through some of the roughest country of all. Driving from dawn to dusk, we covered twelve miles. In a village a man was dying from being bitten in the leg by a jackal; it was too late for amputation, the M.O. said, all he could do was give him some morphine. When we got back to Quetta we had been away two months and I had lost two stones in weight. I was given a fortnight's sick leave. I spent it walking from one meal to the next. After a huge breakfast I would walk to the Club for mid-morning sandwiches and beer and then back to the Mess for lunch. As soon as that was over I began to summon vivid images of tea and dinner.

Perhaps to aid my recovery I was sent on a three weeks' course at the Chemical Warfare School at Pachmarhi in the Central Provinces. This was a stroke of luck financially. Pachmarhi was a long way from Quetta, and at that time officers travelling on duty qualified for various allowances. For a start, you got one and a half times the first class fare, presumably to cope with food and drink en route, and then on top of that you got a by no means negligible sum called a 'Disturbance Allowance'; God knows what that was for—smelling-salts? The result was a considerable profit. Impecunious subalterns were always trying to be sent on a course to some far distant station.

In Pachmarhi the directing staff claimed to have evidence that the Japs had already used gas and planned to use it again. I think that in fact they had no such evidence at all and were merely trying to prevent the course from being considered an utter waste of time. When I went into Burma a year and a few months later we didn't even take our respirators with us, although it is fair to say that the Japs we killed in the Arakan were all carrying theirs. I ran into Tom Berry again at Pachmarhi.

Now that he actually was an officer, and not just officer material, he seemed even more of a caricature, his jaw squarer and his Dunhill briar more firmly fixed, as if welded, into the corner of his mouth. I asked after his wife. "In the pink, old boy, in the pink." Then, with a slight frown: "It was a girl, though. Haven't seen you since the birth, have I? Can't wait to get back and make sure we have a boy as well." There was an implication that his wife had not quite come up to par, giving birth only to a girl: she'd damned well have to get it right next time, after all there was a war on, wasn't there?

When I returned to Quetta we had a new Second-in-Command, a man with a hard expressionless face and two rows of medal ribbons. He eats subalterns for breakfast, I was told. He was trying to knock the unit's drill into shape for a General's inspection. In desperation the next morning I stamped up and down the square, striking sparks from the nails in my boots, bellowing at my squad of Madrassi recruits like Donald Wolfit playing Lear. The Second-in-Command summoned me to his office after the parade. Christ, I thought, I shouldn't have hammed it up as much as that. I'm going to get an imperial ballocking. Instead, he let his features relax almost to a smile. I was the only subaltern in this whole shower who had any feeling at all for drill, he told me. He was putting me in charge of the recruits' drill for the General's parade. All I could do was to continue my ham act. It seemed to impress everyone favourably, including the General. I concluded that square-bashing to an old soldier was like flattery to a woman; you couldn't overdo it.

The C.O. and his wife entertained four of us to dinner one night. Three of us arrived at the stipulated time and were given gins. We waited for the fourth, Major Thompson, a Bertie Wooster type. Thompson had been in the T.A. before the War, and this seemed the only, if not sufficient, reason for his having attained field rank by 1942. In the riding school, when we had to trot without benefit of stirrups, Thompson was always the first to fall off. Once he had fallen off three times in ten minutes, never losing his aimiable grin. The C.O. asked if we knew where he was. We didn't, though we had a fair idea what he would be doing. We were just taking our seats at the dinner table when he arrived, flushed, giggly and talkative. We did our best to keep him out of the conversation, but during the pudding, the inevitable banana fritters, he suddenly got off his chair and crawled under the table. "What on earth's the matter, Thompson?" said the C.O. "Are you feeling all right?" There was no reply, but Thompson could be heard patting the floor and muttering "Oh Christ! Oh Jesus Christ!" "Thompson!" bawled the C.O. "Sir!" Thompson emerged, but remained on all fours. "What the devil are you doing down there?" "I've lost my signet ring, sir. I'm just having a look for it." "Help him find his ring, chaps," said the C.O. wearily. We all padded round the floor, with the exception, of course, of the Colonel and his lady, who remained sitting at each end of the table and tried to make conversation with each other as if nothing out of the ordinary were happening. "Going up to Fort Sandeman next week, my dear." "Oh. Will you be away more than one night?" While they talked above our heads, we whispered urgently to Thompson as we padded round the floor with him, telling him not to be a bloody fool, say he'd found it, anything to stop this suicidal performance. At last he stood up and announced that he was frightfully sorry, but he remembered now, he hadn't been wearing it when he came out. He sat silently while we drank coffee. Before the end of the week he was posted to a unit in Burma.

I missed Thompson. Once I had got drunk with him, for no reason at all. We had been sitting in the Mess after dinner, everyone else out, and Thompson asked the abdar what choice of liqueurs there was. Rather a large choice, it turned out. We sampled all of them. Before we went to bed, Thompson threw a big fat squashy melon high up against the wall. At breakfast he asked innocently what the stain was up there. I kicked him to shut up and told him afterwards he'd done it. "I say, I didn't, did I?" He looked shocked, but only for a moment. Then he giggled. "I say, I do do some extraordinary things, don't I?" I enjoyed his company in Quetta, but I was glad I was never with him in Burma, where it mattered.

In the winter I was posted to Delhi, as a captain.

Temporary Captain

I travelled from Quetta with an Indian officer I'd been friendly with since the Signals School at Mhow. When we changed trains at Lahore, Mehta said he knew two girls, sisters, who lived just outside the town; it might be worth our while to go and see them. We went out in a tonga and I waited while he crept through the dark garden to the girls' bedroom at the back of the house. It was nearly midnight. He came back half an hour later, apologising. Only one of the girls had been there. On the way back to the station he told me that when he was a boy he had tied stones on to his penis to make it grow longer. We slept the rest of the night in the waiting room. Indian station waiting rooms provided cane-bottomed chaises longues for this purpose. The one thing you had to remember was to turn them upside down and beat them to make the bugs fall out.

Mehta was an Indian Christian. Those I knew were nearly all highly sophisticated and emancipated people.

The young ones in particular tended to be not at all religious. To them, being Christian meant no longer being Hindu, and they took full advantage of their freedom from Hinduism's preoccupation with caste and convention. Before we parted Mehta gave me the address of a girl in Delhi called Indira, who was an Indian Christian. I got off the train first. Mehta was going on right across India to Chittagong.

The unit I joined in Delhi was GHQ(I)Signals. It ran the communications for GHQ India. It was all much more advanced technically and on a far larger scale than anything I had come across before. There were teleprinters, and powerful radio transmitters with high diamond-shaped aerials directed on places like Cairo, Calcutta, Colombo and London. Big new installations were being started, and my job was to liaise between, on the one hand, the technical experts in the unit, and, on the other, the various civilian organisations engaged in the work: C.P.W.D. (Central Public Works Department), the Posts and Telegraphs (the Indian equivalent of the Post Office), and the many local contractors hired by the C.P.W.D. to construct offices, workshops, generating stations, erect radio masts and dig ditches for underground cables. The contractors, naturally, were in it for the money, and one of the things I had to do was to see that they did not try to make too much profit by skimping on materials. When they were making a foundation for an aerial mast or a conduit for cable, I would batter at the first part of the work that dried out to see if it would crumble. Most of the day was spent inspecting the several works in progress to make sure that the programme was not falling too far behind time—or being rushed so that the contractor could count on it being too far advanced for him to be told that it wasn't good enough and had to be done again. The Posts and Telegraphs people were mainly Anglo-Indian. They, and the Indian Regiments stationed in Delhi Cantonment, had first-rate hockey teams. We had a match with one or other of them every week, played on a completely grassless 'maidan' of hard, sun-baked earth. The matches began at five o'clock in the afternoon, and in the hot weather, when the temperature even a few hours after dark would still be over 100°F., we came off the pitch with the most raging thirst I have ever known. It was advisable to drink several jugs of iced lime juice before going on to alcohol. If you drank beer or gin and lime too soon, without blunting your thirst beforehand, you could be dead drunk in an hour. The 2i/c, a leather-faced major of many years service out East, liked this to happen once, but only once, to any new officer in the hockey team. He looked sadly at you the next morning and told you you had eyes like pissholes in the snow. We always had plenty of gin in the Mess; the local brand, Carew's, was rather good. Indian whisky was poor. Beer was scarce. Word would come that Wenger's or Davico's had received a consignment of Murree Pilsener, and we would cycle down that evening as soon as work was over; if you didn't go down straightaway you didn't stand a chance, there'd be none the next day. In the Mess we had small, and infrequently delivered, rations of beer. It came from the Solan Brewery and was not up to the standard of Murree Pilsener. Also, there was an idiotic system of supplying the bottles in sacks instead of boxes, so there was a high proportion of breakages in every batch we received.

Our barracks, messes and installations were all in New Delhi, near the overbearingly pompous Secretariat and Viceregal Lodge. The best thing about this grand, imperial architecture was the layout of roads and subsidiary buildings, all of which had spacious borders and gardens with vividly-flowering trees and bushes, jacaranda and 'flame of the forest' and bougainvillaea. On Lodi Road, where we had one of our wireless stations, there were Mogul tombs dotted here and there among the fields. I liked these small-scale, private and usually neglected monuments better than the great showpieces of Mogul architecture. New Delhi had one large, rather pretentious hotel, aptly called The Imperial. There was a good, old-fashioned hotel in Old Delhi called 'Maiden's', not, I believe, to commemorate the chastity of any of its customers or staff, but because a Mr. Maiden had founded it. Between New and Old Delhi, at the side of the railway, was a brothel with a prominent neon sign proclaiming: "Dr. Sultan—Sex Specialist". During the day the girls could be seen sitting out on the balconies, combing their long hair.

The first time I went out with Indira we saw a film about a cartoon elephant called Dumbo. Where did we have dinner? The Imperial? More likely it was at Wenger's or Davico's, nearer to the cinema in Connaught Circus. We went to all of them so many times afterwards, and to Maiden's in Old Delhi, that I cannot now remember which it was that first night. We also went once to another hotel in Old Delhi, but I discovered that they had a rule admitting Indians to the bar and restaurant but not to the swimming pool; this seemed so insultingly nasty that although we didn't want to use the swimming pool I refused to go there again, ever. I liked Maiden's most; it was endearingly frumpish and had 'style', even if it was an out of date style. The Imperial was the best, I suppose, although occasionally the only gin they had was Bols, far too oily if you drank a lot of it. I noticed Mr. Jinnah dining there one night, very much the sharp businessman, I thought—or was it that, Nehru being my hero, I couldn't believe any good of the man who wanted to split India and create a separate Moslem state?

Wherever it was that we dined, I was uncomfortable with Indira that first evening. She looked too glamorous, in a deep-blue sari with a silver border, intricate earrings, umpteen bangles of different colours, and a red spot in the middle of her forehead, and I felt I had to pretend to a degree of sophistication that I didn't have. A few weeks later we sat for hours on Delhi Ridge, in the moonlight, and I took all the hairpins out of her elaborate hair-do. When she went to Mussoorie for a month I decided I was in love with her, so I took a week's leave and followed her up to the hills. She was staying in a YWCA hostel and the woman in charge was extremely suspicious of me when I called; I was a Brutal and Licentious Soldier, that was clear. Indira and I walked in the woods every day. At night we went round and round Mussoorie in a rickshaw, kissing.

Back in Delhi the weather was getting hot. A primitive

kind of air conditioning called 'khas khas tatti' was brought into operation. This consisted of frames of thatch which were fixed into position in place of windows on the side of a building facing the prevailing wind; in the more advanced systems you had a sprinkler pipe running across the top, but if you couldn't afford that, a small boy was hired to sit outside in the heat and throw pails of water over the thatch every few minutes. The wind blew dampened and therefore cooler-feeling air into the room. Our beds were moved out every night into the Mess garden, but even if you slept naked on top of a sheet, with only the mosquito net between you and the sky, you woke up in the early morning your pillow drenched with sweat. The Quartermaster was covered in the pimples of prickly heat; it made me itch whenever I looked at him. He was a tough old soldier, with a face like George Robey's, but although he had been in India for nearly ten years he was in agony from prickly heat every hot weather. A man we called The Mad Major behaved in an even madder way as the temperature rose. He had been seconded to the Signals from an infantry regiment, whose badges he still wore, after inventing a wireless set that had proved particularly effective in operations against the tribes on the North West Frontier. He lived in married quarters in the far corner of the Mess Compound, with his once pretty wife and two small children; in the small hours he could be heard shouting and they weeping. Some evenings he would wander across to the main Mess verandah and sit with us, drinking, most of the time in silence. Suddenly, without relevance to anything said, he would give a high-pitched laugh and shout: "Life is just a bowl of cherries!" Small green parrots flew about the garden. Tree-rats, like miniature, striped squirrels, shot across the grass. In the mornings the muezzin from a nearby mosque sounded more and more querulous. The tail-end of a swarm of locusts descended on us and had to be shovelled up dead the next day, not before they had stripped the trees of most of their foliage. A corporal died of typhoid. We were having jabs every few weeks, against typhoid, cholera, small-pox. Most evenings, after dinner, I walked with Indira to find a patch of not too dried-up grass and we lay for hours, talking, touching, laughing. However hot the weather, her skin always felt cool and tasted of vanilla.

By now, the summer of 1943, there were a lot of Americans in Delhi. We invited some to a Guest Night in the Mess on a day given to celebrating a victory in North Africa. We were going to eat outside and had rigged up coloured lights in the trees. A fat, swarthy Lieutenant with an Italian name and a Bronx accent waved at the garden. "Gee!" he said. "A Guest Night with British awficers, on Toonisia Day—dat's somep'n to write home about!" A few hours later he fell off his chair, drunk, and had to be carried to a waiting jeep.

We had four Rhodesian officers in the unit. One was a Boer, both by ancestry and also in his attitude to those he called "our coloured friends". He was all the more dangerous and detestable, like Enoch Powell today, for his intelligence and insistence on his own integrity and adherence to principle. Two were cheerful extroverts with, apparently, no views about anything except sport, women and "beating it up"; a night out ending in a tonga race would keep them in conversation for a week. The fourth was a quiet, academic type, just qualified as a lawyer before the War started, with liberal enough convictions to provoke the Boer into calling him a traitor to his country and to white people everywhere. Their two sport-loving compatriots would urge them to argument, cheering them on as if watching a cockfight. All four received regularly from their homes in Rhodesia parcels containing 'biltong', strips of dried venison. It was rather good, like savoury chewing gum.

An American film star called Melvyn Douglas, a captain in, I think, their Army Air Force, took Indira out once or twice. I remembered seeing him in some rather funny sophisticated comedies, with people like William Powell and Myrna Loy and Barbara Stanwyck. He was a pleasant chap and by this time I was confident of Indira. I had been very jealous earlier. She had some po-faced Indian Civil Service friends. When I was being catty I told her that they only took her out because it was part of their policy of 'being nice to the natives'. I liked her Indian friends. They used to poke fun at my uniform, urging me to put on a dhoti when Indira and I visited them, telling me how much cooler it was than trousers. I'm sure they were right. Indian dress, loose and flowing, was obviously better than the tight-belted shorts, and boots and puttees, that we wore in the daytime, or the tunic and slacks and shirt with collar and tie that were obligatory at night. English people were silly, they said, bandaging their ankles and tightening their belts. Indira never wore knickers under her sari, just a waist-slip. However, I was still too English to agree to be parted from my trousers in company.

Indira's family were charming. She had two sisters, one older, one younger. The eldest of the three was the one I regarded as most typically Indian. She was plump, placid, kind, serenely beautiful, with a smile like sudden moonlight; she was a good cook, and made a memorable mint chutney. The youngest, still in her teens, was lively, talkative, pretty rather than beautiful. She saw herself, I think, as the 'enfant terrible' of the three. Once, Indira and I were talking to her as she was getting ready for bed. "I'm not going to be the coy Indian maiden in front of you," she said to me, walking about the room with her breasts uncovered. Their mother had been dead a long time. Father was always hospitable and liked to have a gin with me, but I sensed that he was making some effort not to show disapproval that Indira's boy-friend was English, and in the Army, too. They lived in a bungalow near Talkatora Park, about three-quarters of a mile from our Mess. When I walked back in the small hours there were pi-dogs out in the roads, eating the tonga-ponies' droppings. A sweet scent as strong as incense came from a plant called 'lady of the night' in a nearby garden.

The monsoon in Delhi was a half-hearted affair. Rainstorms were better than duststorms, but as the temperature fell humidity grew, and I didn't think the net result was much more comfortable. You could no longer sleep outside, because there would be at least one storm or shower every night, and under a roof, even with fans, it was always sticky. The flying ants were a nuisance, too. The winter months, though, were marvellous: nights cold enough for blankets, early mornings crisp and invigorating, the sun rising in a cloudless sky, and from mid-morning to late afternoon the warmth of a good summer day in England, only drier. In November the installations I had been overseeing were nearly completed. The C.O. said the job would be over by the end of the year. He would see I got a good posting and suggested I might want to go to Burma. I'm not quite sure now what my motives were when I said yes, I would like that. I suspect I was even more ashamed of what the C.O. would think of me if I said no, I would rather go somewhere else, than I was frightened by the prospect of danger and discomfort in the jungle. After the decision had been taken I tried to rationalise it to myself by the thought that it would be both unfair and unfitting to go through a whole war without being involved in actual fighting, but if I could have made the choice without anyone else's knowing I don't suppose the decision would have been the same.

On Christmas Day, after a booze-up in the Sergeants' Mess, the two Rhodesian jokers managed to fit seventeen people in and on to a jeep and drive it a hundred yards before anyone fell off. A few days later I left for Burma. "I've got you into Fifth Indian Division," the C.O. told me. "They know what it's all about. They went right through the Abyssinian campaign." He had a quietly triumphant air, as if he had put me up for Boodle's and prevented my being blackballed. I didn't feel too happy about joining a crowd of battle-scarred veterans; and I felt altogether miserable when I said goodbye to Indira.

An Introduction to Arms

After more than three years in the Army without fighting, I found myself trudging along a jungle path in the middle of the night, the thudding of artillery and the crackling of small arms getting louder all the time. Less alarming noises were the scrape of our own boots, the jingle of harness and the low-gear whine of trucks. The column kept lurching to a halt as, presumably, the Brigadier and his staff conferred on the direction of the path and the probable movements of the Japs. Mules stamped and pissed into the dust. A man had his name taken for lighting a cigarette. The air was so hot and humid that it was almost a relief to be on the move again. At last, the steep upward climb became a steep descent. We were directed off the path and told to off-load. Positions were allocated and a brew of strong sweet tea produced. Sentries were posted on the high ground, and the Adjutant announced that the rest could sleep so long as they kept clothes and boots on.

After leaving Delhi I had had a depressing week in a Transit Camp near Calcutta while some defect in my movement order was sorted out. I had three books with me, chosen partly for convenience of carrying in haversack or pack: *Great Expectations*, *Some Poems* by Auden, and *Les Fleurs du Mal*. The Dickens was particularly good for snapping shut on mosquitoes when they got inside the net. Eventually, first by the slowest and most decrepit train I had ever been in, and then by truck and jeep, I had arrived at Divisional HQ near Maungdaw. This part of the Arakan, between the sea and the Mayu Range, looked scruffy. Strips of jungle spread down from the hills and petered out in thin copses of bamboo. Vehicles moved everywhere in clouds of dust.

True to form, I had not been expected, but stick around, they said, something will turn up. Three days later I was ordered to get out to the Mountain Gunners, up with Nine Brigade. "Alec Mackenzie's bought a nasty one. Shell splinter through the mouth. That's the end of his war. Well, you'll see some fireworks with that mob, and all on your flat feet, too. Better than being arse-bound, eh?"

The Mountain Gunners' RHQ command post had been cut out of a hillside, with a few tree-trunks and a tarpaulin for a roof. The Adjutant, 'Chink' Charrington, was polite and affable; his eyes were slightly slanting and turned into thin slits when he laughed. The Second-in-Command, tall and rangy, always chewing twigs or stalks of grass, looked incredibly young and at the same time weather-beaten, more like a teenage cowboy than an Indian Army major. There was a fat, jolly Indian

Doctor with a long Madrassi name, a fierce-looking but mild-mannered Sikh Intelligence Officer, and the only Quartermaster I ever met who wasn't an old soldier; he had been an accountant in civil life, with a nice house in Chislehurst. The men were all Sikhs or Punjabi Musselmen. The guns were 3.7 howitzers, the original screw guns; they had a short range, a high trajectory, and great accuracy. They were carried on enormous mules. These came from the Argentine, according to the Quartermaster, and were extremely valuable, one animal costing more than a jeep. "The C.O.'s very hot on mules. If you let one go lame he won't half give you a rocket."

I was introduced to the C.O., who questioned me vigorously. None of my answers seemed to allay his suspicions that the Regiment had been sent a dud. Delhi was the worst possible place to have come from, full of General Staff and Civil Servants. Oxford was famous for not wanting to die for King and Country, and to have spent the first year of the War there reading Latin and Greek and philosophy was effete to the nth degree. A slight knowledge of Urdu gave a little hope that I might not be entirely useless, but the C.O. left no doubt that he saw standards dropping fast when people like me were wished on the Mountain Artillery. Later, when the C.O. had gone to bed, the Adjutant "put me in the picture". The C.O. was a prickly customer when things were quiet; during what was called a "show", he was happy, good-tempered and considerate. Things had been suspiciously quiet for a week or two, and his temper had become very frayed. "Give him Yes and No answers and stay out of his way as much as humanly possible, old boy."

Things had continued quiet for a few days. "Must be damned irritating, eh, to come all this way from Delhi and find nothing much happening?" The C.O. glared. I agreed, hoping I had given my "Yes, indeed, Sir!" the right amount of enthusiasm.

Then one morning the C.O. had returned from Div. HQ looking positively cheerful. "The balloon's gone up on the other side of the Range," he announced. "The Brigade's going over the pass tonight. Move off nineteen hundred hours. Just what you've been waiting for, eh, Jack? Wireless silence, though. The Japs are all over the place, it seems."

After a little less than two hours' sleep we were up for the dawn stand-to. Trenches were dug, water and rations given out, mules groomed, sentries changed, batteries put on charge, feet washed, equipment checked. I went with my party of linesmen as they laid a line to Brigade HQ. It was not far but across a hollow where the jungle was thick and we had to cut a way through the vegetation. It was very hot all day. It seemed to get even stickier when at last the sun went down behind the hills we had marched over. One's training as a cadet at Bangalore, mainly on a flat, sandy plain, scarred with dried-up water-courses, and then as a subaltern, with squads of bemused recruits, on the even drier, rockier hills round Quetta, where you could go for miles and never see a tree, did not seem to me to have been the best of preparations for jungle warfare.

With the darkness the Jap shelling started, but we were tucked under the brow of a hill and most of the shells went over us. In the small hours came orders to move. Confusion, or so it appeared to me, broke out again. Also, it rained, and though it was refreshing to feel it on face and arms and shoulders, the dust on the tracks was quickly changed to mud, and marching was twice the effort. Soon, sweat and rain were indistinguishable.

We were in our new position by first light, and the rain stopped. An hour later, trenches dug and sentries posted, we ate breakfast. After tea and bacon, time to stand in the sun and smoke a cigarette. Then—an ear-splitting racket, and the mess-cook, who had also been sunning himself a few yards away, fell, made a gargling, bubbling sound, lay obviously dead. I threw myself flat on the ground, under a bush. Men ran, shouted, cowered. I should be doing something. But what? A West Yorks sergeant and two men ran past towards the firing and I followed them up the hill to the crest. The Sikh sentry was dead in his trench. His telephone still worked. The sergeant proposed a target and I passed this down the phone to RHQ. The two West Yorks privates fired their rifles hopefully. The howitzers opened up. After a few minutes there was silence again. Nothing from the Japs. The Adjutant rang. We were to move again. Near the command post, I saw a party digging the mess-cook's grave.

The C.O. was in high spirits. The Japs were attacking all round, and the Brigade was to fall back a couple of miles and form a Box. There was a rumour that the General commanding the Division to which we were now attached had escaped in his pyjamas when his HQ had been over-run in the night. When we had formed the Box and organised perimeter defences, we were to stand fast and give no more ground. Ammunition and rations would be dropped by parachute. To be surrounded no longer mattered, Mountbatten had declared; we had his guarantee that the air-drop would supply us with everything we needed for as long as we needed it. The situation could not have been more to the C.O.'s liking. He called me 'old boy' for the first time.

Several hours later, in the heat of the afternoon, I was plodding up a track to our new position with a party of linesmen and mules. I had taken off my steel helmet and hung it from my belt; my head felt like a steamed pudding. The C.O. drove past in his jeep. He waved excitedly. "This is better than Delhi, eh, Jack?" Delhi! Where the bars in Connaught Circus had Murree Pilsener beer. Another "Yes, indeed, Sir!"

The Box was formed by sunset. Chink Charrington went round allocating defence responsibilities for sections of the perimeter with the air of a vicar issuing invitations to look after stalls at a village fête. The Doctor set up his Aid Post. The mules were put under whatever cover could be found. I filled my water bottle with rum. It grew dark. We waited.

First, the Jap shelling started. Then, yelling and screaming, and firing tracer, their infantry attacked, but the noise they made and the sight of their tracer bullets gave away their movements so clearly that none of them got through. They tried again later, more stealthily, but with no more success. By midnight they had settled for desultory mortaring and shelling. I was so exhausted, and had drunk so much rum, that I fell asleep when the shelling stopped and had to be woken up for the dawn stand-to.

Not many men had been killed, but some were badly wounded. As more and more casualties were brought in, a sweet and sickening smell spread from the Regimental Aid Post. Chink decided that several of the wounded mules had to be shot. He ordered their livers to be taken out before they were buried. "Might as well have a good meal tonight," he remarked. It took a lot of digging to bury a dead mule, and it all had to be done inside the Box. The ground remained spongy for the rest of the time we were there, and the stench would seep through the earth every now and then.

We were cut off for two weeks. Every night the Japs built an observation post in a tall tree on a rise overlooking the Box. Every morning one of the howitzers, fired over open sights, shot it down; men and pieces of wood tumbled to the ground.

On the fifth morning a Jap sniper killed Chink Charrington as he was inspecting the sentry posts. The toecaps of his boots shone in the sun as we put him in a grave. One of the Battery Captains, Maurice Hilton, was made Adjutant. Where Chink had been small and neat and urbane, Maurice was large and hairy and loquacious. When he sat he sprawled.

Maurice was superstitious. After a day or two he noticed that as soon as I got into the few inches of water in my canvas bath, a Jap shell or mortar bomb would fall near the command post. "I wonder, old chap," he said, "if you'd mind not having baths until we get this little lot sorted out. It does seem to spark things off rather."

One night a party of Japs, talking and laughing as if they had no idea where they were, came up the path by the side of the stream that flowed into and through the Box. The sentries, West Yorks on one side of the stream, the Regiment's Sikhs on the other, let them approach within a few yards and then opened fire. In the morning seventeen Jap bodies were counted. Most of them had fallen in the stream, our only water supply. The Doctor put so much chlorine in the drinking water we took from it in the next day or two that it was only with the addition of large amounts of rum that we could bring ourselves to swallow it, even in tea. The Japs were found to be carrying wads of specially printed rupee notes for use in the India they planned to conquer. Also in their pockets were photographs of wives and children and some very fat and unsavoury nudes. It was assumed that the men were reinforcements who had been remarkably bad map readers, or, perhaps more likely, had taken for granted that their original plan of attack had worked and our positions had been over-run. In either case, how they had failed to contact their own troops besieging the Box remained a mystery. Perhaps the encircling troops were thinning out.

The supply drops were so good that we always had enough to eat. The food was mostly tinned stew, made more interesting by the addition of varying amounts of curry powder; bully beef, straight, fried or hashed; tinned bacon; and chapatis; always with strong, sweet tea, laced with rum. There was in fact unlimited rum, the whole twelve months I was with the Mountain Gunners. The Quartermaster had originally indented for a rum ration for the total number of men in the Regiment, even though half of them, being Mohammedan, did not drink. He had judged it best to go on ordering the same quantity, in the hope that his initial error, and current policy, would go undetected until the War was over.

I was learning. What had at first been a banging, crashing chaos could be sorted out now into ours and theirs, field guns and howitzers, mortars and grenades, machine guns, tommy guns and rifles. Certain sights and sounds and smells no longer made me feel sick or angry or dispirited, and at the time this all seemed as it should be; survival was more important than sensitivity. I never knew for sure whether I killed anyone. I shot often enough with a rifle at shadowy moving figures, but there was no means of checking who had killed whom. I have never felt any qualms at all about being either directly or indirectly responsible for killing Japanese soldiers in Burma. It was a straight case of Them or Us, and I was for Us. I think I would have been upset if I had been involved in the destruction of cities and civilians that went on in Europe. We were lucky in the jungle that there were hardly any solid buildings to destroy and that the few inhabitants could easily keep out of the way. Also, it was an egalitarian warfare; ambushes, 'hooks' and hit-and-run raids made everyone a combatant, put everyone at risk, from Divisional HQ forward.

Towards the end of the second week there were signs that the Japs were running short of ammunition and food. One quiet afternoon two Sikhs were washing their hair when an exhausted Jap wriggled out of the bushes and tried to drag away a sack of dried vegetables. They turned on him and killed him, breaking his neck with their hands. The wretched man looked thin to the point of emaciation. The Sikhs laughed and went back to combing out their almost waist-length hair.

A few days later the Japs decided they had lost this battle. They just abandoned their positions one night, leaving evidence that they had been suffering badly from diarrhoea.

The Regiment marched back over the pass in daylight and rejoined our own Division. There was a rumour that we were going to be taken out for a rest. The C.O. grew more and more ill-tempered at the prospect. Then, one evening, he returned from Div. HQ all smiles. Things were boiling up on the borders of Assam and Manipur. We were to march back to an airstrip, about 120 miles north, from where we would be flown, guns, mules and all, to this new 'tamasha'. The name of Kohima was mentioned as our probable destination. The march to the airstrip was to begin the next evening and was to take five nights. "Soap socks tomorrow night, gentlemen," said the C.O. "With a bit of luck we'll be in action again in not much more than a week."

The Flaming Arsehole

At the side of the airstrip was the fuselage of an old Dakota, on which we practised loading. We hedged each side of a ramp with leafy branches to persuade the mules that they were regaining the Argentinian paradise they might have thought for ever lost. Some were not fooled and remained immobile, indifferent to thwacks and curses. Then came an order that we were not to take the mules with us after all. The first plane to fly some had nearly crashed when the mules pissed and short-circuited the electrical system in the aircraft. We were to go into action with jeeps instead, and the mules would go round by road and rail and join us later.

American crews flew us over the mountains to Dimapur. They were a laconic lot. Tell your men No Smoking, the captain said; that done, they lit up Chesterfields and read lurid-looking comics. I explained to my men, Punjabi peasants most of them and flying for the first time, that Americans were mad but safe pilots. There were no doors on the plane and no seats, and when we banked sharply those of us near the door-space on the lower side had to brace our feet against the fuselage and hang on to our rifles and equipment to avoid an impromptu air-drop.

The other two Brigades in the Division were flown to Imphal. We drove in lorries, trucks and jeeps from Dimapur up the Manipur Road to Kohima. Kohima was a straggle of low buildings where the road passed over a ridge five thousand feet high. It dominated the road back to the railhead and airstrip at Dimapur and forward to the Imphal Plain. The Japs were said to be converging on it fast from two or three directions, but it was a good position to defend. Then came what the Adjutant described bitterly as "a complete fucking fuck-up". We were ordered back down to Dimapur. Our Brigadier was rumoured to be livid and to have demanded to see Slim, even Mountbatten, if this bloody silly order were not changed. It was. We rushed back up the road, but we had lost our advantage. The Japs were at each end of the Kohima Ridge already. We managed to get a battalion of the Royal West Kents and one of the Regiment's Batteries on the middle of the ridge before the Japs closed in. The rest of us formed another Box a mile or two back at Jatsoma, where we were cut off in our turn by the Japs. A good defensive position had been thrown away, said our C.O., because some damn-fool General in charge of a shower of L. of C. clerks had had us going up and down the road like bloody yo-yos when we might have made ourselves impregnable; now a lot of people would die who needn't have.

He was right. After a week or two the ridge began to look like a scene from the Western Front in the Great War. Tall pines were stripped of their branches by shell-fire and cut to the status of stunted olive trees and vines in winter. The few trees that survived were festooned with parachutes from the supply drop. A Lance-Corporal in the West Kents won a posthumous V.C. Our 'cowboy' Second-in-Command was killed by a direct hit from a mortar bomb. One wet afternoon I helped to carry Naik Aurangzeb Khan down the muddy hillside on a stretcher. He had a fairly neat wound through his thigh. When the road was opened and he was sent back to hospital he made me give him a letter insisting that when he was O.K. he be posted back to us. Without that, he said, those Base-wallahs might post him to any old unit. (It worked, too, and a couple of months later he returned to us.)

Our Box at Jatsoma was relieved first, by a British Division. We'll take over the defensive fire on to the ridge, their Gunners said condescendingly; let's have a dekko at the target. When they learned that we'd been firing on to the far side of a tennis court in the District Commissioner's garden, with our own troops on the near side, night and day for ten days, once firing over three thousand rounds in five hours, and never causing a single casualty among our own troops, they said we'd better carry on, their 25-pounders couldn't quite cope with that.

It took another three weeks to clear the Japs from Kohima. Their utter lack of regard for their own lives was, I thought, not just insane but obscenely so. One badly wounded man in a bunker, squashed in a pile of corpses, everything round him destroyed, would go on firing his machine gun or throwing grenades until he was buried in débris. In one place, when the last man had been killed, the Sappers had to bulldoze the bodies away; they had become a foul-smelling 'mush', fly-blown and indivisible.

The C.O. wrote flowery letters to our casualties' next of kin, most of them in the Punjab and North West Frontier Province, a few in the U.P. He wrote the same letter for a man killed by a sack of grain during an air-drop. Now the road was open the men had their first 'meat on hoof' for weeks, a lorry-load of goats, bleating pathetically as they were led off to be killed. The men invited me to eat with them that night; the curried goat was excellent. The next day we went on to Imphal to join the rest of our Division. I told my Havildar, Mohammed Aslam, that I was recommending him for promotion to Jemadar. We were all cock-a-hoop at the Kohima victory and one man asked for leave to go home and marry a second wife, but I told him that luxuries like second wives would have to wait until we'd chased the Japs a bit further away from India.

Most of us had diarrhoea or dysentery from time to time, and Indira sent me cigarette tins full of a mysterious powder which was supposed to have a constipating effect. One of the Battery Captains remarked proudly that his shit had been the colour and consistency of strawberry ice cream for several weeks. Another returned from leave complaining that he'd looked forward to proper lavatories but had found he didn't enjoy it any more sitting down.

Mountbatten came to visit us. We were going to be taken out for a rest, everyone said. Mountbatten sprang out of a jeep, looking like a film star. We'd had a bad time in the Arakan, and Kohima and Imphal had been even worse, he ought to be able to send us out of things for a bit, but he needed a Division to push on in the monsoon along the Tiddim Road, up the Chocolate Staircase to Kennedy Peak and Fort White, winkling out the Japs as they went, and there was only one Division he knew he could entrust that job to . . . di dah di dah di dah.

I had a month's leave. On my way to Delhi I stopped a night in Calcutta. Our Divisional emblem, or 'flash', was a red circle in a black square, known in the Fourteenth Army as 'the flaming arsehole'. In the bars along Chowringhee when people saw this on my sleeve they came up and asked what it had been like at Imphal and Kohima. There was a nasty temptation to load one's "Oh, not too bad, really" with pregnant understatement.

Indira was waiting on the platform at Delhi. It was her birthday. Her father, bless him, raised no objection to our going away together. We went to Naini Tal, a hill station with a lake and hotels and bars, in one of them draught beer. We rowed on the lake and walked up hills between massive banks of rhododendrons. It was cold at night and we splashed each other in a tin bath. In the mornings men appeared on the verandah outside our room selling big baskets of flowers. We said we'd get married when the War was over. At the end of the holiday we went down by car to Bareilly Junction.

Indira got into the train to Delhi. When it moved off I ran along the platform holding her hand. Then I got the train going the other way.

There was a new C.O. when I got back. Unlike his predecessor this one thought the sun shone out of my arse. He took me with him, not an Artillery officer, when we went on 'hooks' to come up behind the Japanese. On one of these we lay up for a day in a Chin village. The Chins had great earthenware jars, as big as themselves, full of rice beer. They gave a party and we drank the rice beer out of old pineapple-chunk tins; everybody got pissed, and we danced in a big circle, arms linked with the tiny Chin women, moving with a slow, shuffling step, first one way, then the other, to a monotonous, grunting song. We were still drunk when we moved off in the middle of the night, and it was a wonder that the Japs didn't hear us coming.

We had a new Second-in-Command, too: Richard de Courtenay Yeo. He had been very brave at Kohima, winning the D.S.O., but I thought of him as an endearing innocent. It was impossible to make him observe wireless security; in fact, after a while, I had to tell him not to bother, it was worse when he tried. He would come on the air from an O.P. and say: "The Fourth/Seventh Rajputs are moving to—Oh Lord, I shouldn't have said that, should I? What the hell's the Rajputs' code name? Oh, I've got it—Bolo. Yes. Bolo are moving to . . ."

We went on and on up the Tiddim Road. There was an outbreak of scrub typhus as we passed through an area of elephant grass. One of our Battery officers got it and died. The prescribed treatment was rest and quiet and careful nursing, and there wasn't much chance of any of that.

After a time I couldn't see the War ending for years and years. There was still most of Burma to fight through, and then there'd be Malaya and Singapore and Siam and God knew where else, culminating, it had to be supposed, in an air- and sea-borne invasion of Japan. I wrote to Indira, calling it off. My batman was depressed, too. He was a registered opium eater and received more or less regular supplies through the R.I.A.S.C., but he was dissatisfied with the quality; it had got worse and worse lately, he complained. His efficiency always dropped alarmingly if he wasn't getting the right quantity or quality of opium, so I sent him on leave to Peshawar to let him stock up with the real McCoy.

Occasionally we had a two or three day rest, but being the only Mountain Gunners in the Division we were usually hard at it. During the rests we had the crimes passionnels. One Sikh would fire at and wound another Sikh for moving in on his paramour. All three, as often as not, were married men with families back in the Punjab; they took their sex where they could find it, and in the hills and jungle of Burma they could only find it in one another. We always falsified the documentation of the court of inquiry, to make it seem that the tommy gun had gone off by accident. There was no sense in demoting a good N.C.O. merely because he had had a fit of sexual jealousy over a spot of sodomy.

It wasn't all danger and depression and dysentery, of course, by any manner of means. For one thing, there was breathtakingly beautiful scenery. I wouldn't advise a coach tour of the Arakan, but the mountains of Manipur and Nagaland and the Chin Hills are spectacular. Immense valleys, ten miles wide and three or four thousand feet deep, changed from green to every shade of blue and purple as the sun went down. Most of the time we were climbing up and down these hillsides and valleys, so we were very fit, fitter, I suppose, for my part, than I have ever been in my life before or since, and that in itself is a pleasant sensation. And we fashioned some amusements. Poker was the most usual. I was winning quite a lot once, more than a hundred rupees, when the C.O. came back into the Mess and watched for ten minutes; then he declared the game null and void on the grounds that one of the players, who had just come in from an O.P., was shell-shocked. One of the Batteries had an old gramophone and a few records. I remember having supper with them one night, on the bank of a rushing stream we had just forded, and then drinking tea and rum and listening to the Ink Spots. At least, I think it was the Ink Spots. The tune I know for certain. It was Java Jive: "I like coffee, I like tea, I like a Java Jive and it likes me." A subaltern called Gulab Khan was in the party. He shouldn't have drunk any alcohol at all, being a Mohammedan, but he drank as much as any of us. His one concession to orthodoxy was that during Ramadan he didn't drink before the sun had definitely set; in the evenings the rest of us would start on rum in the Mess while Gulab Khan nursed his, untouched, until his batman, stationed on a rise up with the sentries, shouted to him that it was O.K., the sun was below the horizon.

There was a Mountain Artillery song, to the tune of the Eton Boating Song. I can only remember snatches: "You can run if you please, you can climb up the trees, but you can't get away from the guns. Oh, we all love the screw guns . . ." And there was a reference to the long-eared mules: "with the khachhas' ears all flapping."

In December we were at last taken out for a rest and refit, in a genuine 'pyjama area'. The Adjutant had three classifications of places when it came to sleeping: boots on, boots off, and, when there was no conceivable liklihood of Japs popping up, a pyjama area. For a month or two we would be able to get undressed every night when we went to bed. I promptly got malaria and spent a couple of weeks in hospital.

The Last Christmas

Birkinshaw was just getting out of the bath when I arrived. Still wet, wearing a bath towel like a sarong, he advanced into the middle of the bedroom, into which I had been summoned as to a monarch's levée. The bearer handed his sahib a large whisky; then, as Birkinshaw revolved slowly under the slightly faster-revolving ceiling fan, he patted him dry with a towel and shook talcum powder over him. Adequately dried for social intercourse, Birkinshaw shook my hand. Yes, I looked like Claude's son, he said. Chatting about my father, the jute industry, the Bengal Club—"Sorry to have asked you your rank on the telephone, but if you hadn't been an officer I couldn't have had you here for dinner in the Club"—he was ceremoniously dressed. He took no part himself in this operation, except to hold out the appropriate foot, leg or arm for the bearer to insert it into sock, trouser or shirt. There was never a false or unnecessary move. It was like the pas de deux from a ballet long established in the repertoire. Only when it came to the tieing of the tie did Birkinshaw take over; that was sahib's work, evidently. At last, resplendent in white dinner jacket and red cummerbund, Birkinshaw was ready for the second large whisky.

It was just before Christmas. From our rest area near Kohima, where eight months before we had been cut off by the Japs, I had been sent to Calcutta, with one Sikh and one Punjabi Musselman N.C.O., to buy what were rather childishly called 'comforts' for the Regiment. Naiks Manohar Singh and Mohammed Akbar were finding it easy enough to get the shampoos and coconut oil, the spices and Indian whisky and cheap cigarettes they were detailed to take back, and I had got hams and chutneys and shaving creams and pipes and tobacco; but I'd had no joy looking for the real Scotch whisky and French brandy I'd been urged to obtain at, almost, any cost. "Not a hope, mate, in this benighted fucking city" had been the answer when I asked around in the bar of the Grand Hotel. "You can bet your boots the jutewallahs have got their hands on it if there is any." That had given me the idea of looking up my father's old school friend, Birkinshaw.

In the dining-room, beneath immense portraits of John Company dignitaries, Viceroys, and Governors of Bengal, we ate large quantities of magnificent roast beef. There was a superb Stilton cheese. And a very good port. My appetite earned the notice, and approving comment, of my host. "I must say, Jack, you seem to be pretty fit after all that time in the jungle. I like to see a young chap enjoy his food and drink—so long as he can hold it, of course, without making a fool of himself." Red in the face, Birkinshaw became fulsome in his compliments. "I must write to old Claude and tell him his son's in good form. Fathers like to hear about it when their sons have turned up trumps. Only had a daughter myself. Well, let's go and see if there's anyone in the billiards room, and have another drink there."

There was one white-haired old man, playing against himself. When I was introduced he looked at my green battledress and divisional flash. "So you're with that crowd, are you? Expect it's pretty bad out there at times, eh? We've had it pretty bad here too in Calcutta. Oh yes. Yes indeed. There have been times when we couldn't get Black Label for love or money. Just wasn't any to be had anywhere, anywhere at all."

We brooded silently on this drastic state of affairs for a few minutes, and then I judged it to be the right moment to sound Birkinshaw about the possibility of obtaining Scotch and Cognac. For the first time the jutewallah showed in him. "You won't get anything like that on credit, you know. Can you pay cash?" "Yes, I can, actually." "That's all right, then. Not to worry. I can make a bandobast with the Club's supplier. A case of each do you? Give me a ring tomorrow midday. I'll have it for you."

It was a short walk back along Chowringhee to the Grand Hotel. In the bar three or four tables had been put together and a party of about twelve, their kit scattered at their feet, were obviously going to make a night of it before catching the early morning train.

One of them threw back his head and howled. It sounded like a party piece, the imitation of a jackal or just a lament for a finished leave, but it went on and on as his friends got up and carried him out. "DTs," said one of the party. "That's the third time. He always starts like that."

Two days later we were on our way back with 27 wooden boxes, all carefully packed and an identifying number stencilled on their sides. The journey to Dimapur involved two changes of train and a ferry crossing of the Brahmaputra. One of the two N.C.O.s was always to be in the van with the boxes.

There were four Gurkha subalterns in the compartment. They compared, in vivid detail, the Calcutta brothels with those of Bombay and Lahore. An old Captain Quartermaster advised them, next time, to get themselves a rubber woman and fill her with hot marmalade. There seemed to be a brand of humour peculiar to quartermasters. Tubby Webster in Delhi. Whenever you went into his stores to ask for another drum of cable or new batteries his answer was always "Sorry, old sport, haven't got any, not a sausage, but you can put your cock in my ear and wiggle it about a bit!"

It was pitch-black at Dimapur, and there was the usual Indian station hubbub, even though nearly all the passengers were military, on their way back from leave or hospital to the Burma front or the Manipur Road L. of C. The guard had promised not to signal the train's departure until everything was out, but there were still eight boxes in the van when the train gave a lurch and moved forward. As it gathered speed, Mohammed Akbar panicked and jumped down on to the platform. Where was the guard, for Christ's sake? He approached, sheepishly. "Sahib, I stay here in Dimapur. Is new guard on train now. I am telling him, sahib, but he is not listening." We watched the rear lights of the train fade into the distance as it puffed away north to the Assam tea gardens.

The rest of the night was like a second-feature movie. A shed at the side of the station entrance housed the R.T.O., an elderly captain who looked up startled from the Penguin edition of *A Farewell to Arms.* Vital stores and equipment for my Regiment had been left on the train to Jorhat. Must have a truck to follow it and get them back. I signed for a 15-cwt.

The trouble with the road, apart from its uneven, stony surface, was that it looped away from the railway to converge only at the next station. The train had been and left, still, it was to be assumed, with the boxes. The same thing happened at the next five halts; 'station' was too grand a word for an earth ramp and one or two wooden huts with corrugated iron roofs. The sky was lightening when we arrived at last at one of these places at the same time as the train, The guard and a minute stationmaster helped to unload the boxes. Guard, driver, stationmaster and Manohar Singh accepted whisky from my water-bottle and we sat around drinking out of chipped and dirty cups. Guard and stationmaster, both explained, were not supposed to touch alcohol, but in view of the crisis brilliantly averted were prepared to stretch a point. The train whistled long and, it seemed, drunkenly, as it moved off.

We were back in the unit lines by dusk. The enormous valley was full of purple shadow. "I didn't know there was so much good hooch in the whole of India," said the Adjutant, admiringly. "And cigars, Jamaican cigars! You didn't bring any women back, by any chance, did you?" " 'A woman is only a woman, but a good cigar is a smoke', " said the C.O. He had the habit of quoting Kipling whenever the opportunity presented itself, in order to show these young officers who had *New Writing* sent out to them that he was not altogether uncultured.

Christmas Eve was spent with the Sikhs, getting drunk on Indian whisky, Christmas Day first in the R.H.Q. Mess, then in each of the three Battery Messes, getting drunk on Scotch. It was a good Christmas, the last Christmas of the War.

Time-Expired Man

We were shifted from our original rest area on the Manipur Road to a new position in the tea gardens near Jorhat. Jorhat was a Somerset Maugham town. The rich planters frequented the Club. The not-so-rich, and there were many more of them, went to tatty cafés and restaurants. It had not occurred to me that for every one successful white entrepreneur out East there were several who could barely keep their heads above water. They preserved certain genteel airs, but they seemed faded, secretive, even sinister, as if all that was left to them for pleasure was to indulge, in private, in unmentionable practices. The women all looked like Bette Davis in her more macabre roles. Unlike the successful, who could afford to be jolly and hospitable, the poor whites appeared to resent the intrusion of soldiers into their drab and sullen lives. When we held a Divisional race meeting—at which I won quite a large sum by betting on one of my men in the mule race—they wandered among the crowd like ghosts, aloof both from us and from their own loud-voiced, red-faced oligarchs. I was sorry for them, but there seemed no point of contact and any attempt to make one would have provoked, I am sure, a snub. They gave the impression that they were just waiting for us to go away and leave them in the rut to which they had become resigned, making enough to live but not enough to enjoy any of the sahib's prerogatives, unable to keep up with the Joneses but regarding it as unthinkable to mix with the Prem Naths.

I had now had a year with the Mountain Gunners, and before we went back into action I was moved to a job in Div. HQ. I had mixed feelings about this. I liked the Gunners, felt flattered to have been accepted by them, had made many friends. I liked their life, too, curiously enough. It was physically hard, often exciting, rarely free from danger; the catchphrase, 'never a dull moment', just about summed it up. And there was all that rum. At the same time, I couldn't help feeling relief. There had been a lot of casualties in the Regiment during the year, and the realisation that there would now be less chance of my being wounded or killed was undoubtedly comforting. Apart from malaria and diarrhoea, I had suffered nothing worse than a broken wristwatch when I took a header into a slit trench to avoid a dive-bomber that seemed to be coming straight at me, and I didn't think that luck like that could last for ever. Also, it meant getting my third pip back.

There were several farewell parties. I worked on a flowery speech in Urdu so that I could reply not too inadequately to the Subedar-Major's speech. I received several presents: a tiny suitcase, an Indian Silver cigarette case, and an identity disc on a chain necklace. I was encouraged to get spectacularly drunk.

When we went back into Burma it was to the flat and dusty central plain, quite different from the jungle-covered mountains we had been fighting in before. My new job meant that I was usually a few miles behind the actual fighting, and everything seemed much more boring. At last the Japs began to retreat faster and faster. We were going hell-for-leather down the Rangoon Road when my repatriation order came through. I asked if I could put it off for a month. After all that mucking about in obscure hills and forests I thought it would make a change to enter the capital city of a re-conquered country. Girls would throw flowers at us, invite us to their soft, silk-sheeted beds. Bars would serve free drinks. Churchill would make a speech: our victorious troops, once known as the Forgotten Army, yesterday returned in triumph, etc. No, they said. You can forego it altogether for another four years, or go now. I went then.

Indira had become engaged to someone else, but we went together to stay with her now married elder sister in Jhansi. It was very hot, and one afternoon we were all sprawled on mattresses under the big ceiling fan. Indira's father and I were in pyjamas. He examined my feet. "You have slim feet for an Englishman," he said; "they could be an Indian's feet." Now he tells me, I thought. When I left to catch my train to Deolali, near Bombay, I scraped my shin on my tin trunk as I was getting into the tonga, so I didn't know if I was crying at leaving Indira or whether it was just that my eyes were watering in reaction to the pain in my leg.

At Deolali I met a friend from 5 Div. going home on the same draft. Len was the best poker and liar dice player I had ever met. He drank a lot, too. One afternoon we stencilled our trunks and cases, marking them Wanted On Voyage or Not Wanted On Voyage but forgetting to let the paint dry on the top before we turned them to stencil the sides. The result, we decided, was an interesting development in the uses of distortion, and we invited our neighbours in the camp to admire our handiwork and share the Cypriot brandy that had inspired it. The next morning we did it all again, legibly.

As the ship moved away from the quay thousands of men sang 'A Troopship was leaving Bombay, bound for old Blighty's shore, heavily laden with time-expired men, bound for the land they adore', and there was no nonsense about 'Bless 'em all'. A fervent 'Fuck 'em all' roared across the harbour. It was the Cup Final to end all Cup Finals, the Last Trump. "Roll on, that boat," everyone had said for four years, and now it was rolling, and they were on it. The war in Europe was over, so we came back through the Canal. In Port Said nobody was allowed off the ship and there were lurid stories of what we were missing in the dives and brothels. Everybody knew somebody who knew somebody else who had actually seen the donkey and the woman. Len was impatient to get home and sire a child before his forty-year-old wife was past it. I told him hot baths were emasculating, and he had cold sea water showers every day, even as we approached the Clyde. The lascar crew stole the cigarette case and identity disc necklace my troops had given me, and when I was packing to get off the ship their tiny suitcase disintegrated.

We were taken by train to a camp near Thirsk and given rail warrants for disembarcation leave. Then they drove us into the middle of Thirsk and left us. We examined the pubs in the Market Square and chose one. "What are you having, Jack?" "Oh, a pint of bitter, I think, Len." Big moment. I changed trains at Leeds and rang up my mother to tell her I'd be home for tea. Outside Huddersfield Station I thought first of getting a taxi but pre-war custom asserted itself and I lugged my case down to the trolley-bus stop. I felt a bit daft now, wearing a bush-hat with the flaming arsehole on it and a Fourteenth Army flash on my sleeve. Nobody here would know what they were. They might even think I was Australian.

Coal, of course, had been rationed during the War and my father's job had folded. He was now working for a firm in Brighouse, as not much more than a clerk. He had come down in the world, and his appearance reflected this. I had always thought of him as a smartly dressed man. I could remember him wearing grey spats. Now he had a shapeless, not too clean, belted gaberdine raincoat; he wore it on all occasions, whatever the weather and temperature. It was quite a warm summer, and he would arrive home in the evening sweating and looking crumpled. I suggested he didn't need his coat, but he insisted it was necessary. "Saves your suit on the buses, son," he said. His suit didn't look as if it had been saved. I was sorry for him and felt guilty about my intention to vote Labour in the Election, because if Labour got in the mines would be nationalised and his old job would be gone for ever. Labour did get in, but it wasn't with the help of my vote. I discovered that the registration forms we had filled in months and months ago in Burma had not been received in time. The same had happened to other people I knew who had just returned from overseas, and there was talk of a conspiracy by the establishment to reduce what was expected to be a big Servicemen's vote for Labour.

I was posted to Catterick. Len was there, too. Among his various talents was the ability to play the piano seductively. Early one evening in the as yet apparently deserted Club he bet me he could play the grand piano in the ballroom so that within ten minutes he would have a woman talking to him. He launched into the Warsaw Concerto. Within five minutes a woman appeared in the gallery which encircled the room. She listened, in a dreamy attitude, for two minutes, then came down the stairs and went over to the piano. Len stopped playing. "That was lovely," she said. "Do you know any more Tchaikovsky?" There had been an American major in Delhi who at dances would go up to a girl he didn't know, but wanted to, stare at her for a few moments and then say, slowly and in a pronounced Southern drawl, "Are you gonna dance with me or are you not?" Almost invariably he danced away with her. It seemed to me that the art of the pick-up called for some hypnotic power which I did not possess. Just after VJ Day my malaria came back. When the fever had gone down I was given Guinness, "to restore the red corpuscles," the Sister said, and was encouraged to go to the Club for an hour or two each evening to add my own quota to this restorative régime. I went home for a fortnight's sick leave, but before it was over the Adjutant rang me up. Would I care to go to York the next day and get demobbed? My Class B Release had come through in time for me to go back to Oxford in October.

Yes, I said, I would.

Where I Came In

The subject of my first essay was something to do with Plato's theory of ideal forms, and in the course of it I mentioned 'numbers'. MacKinnon stopped me dead: "What IS a number?" I thought, but not for long. Army training had demanded quick decisions, even wrong decisions being judged better than none at all or than those arrived at slowly. "It's something like the shape of a relationship," I said. "I see." Pause. "I SEE." He was a big man, with a disconcerting stare and a resonant, nasal voice. The words he wished to emphasize, and they were many, were boomed out as through a loud hailer. "And yet, and YET, I have many mathematicians among my friends, and they all ASSURE ME, they ALL FEEL, that they are dealing with ACTUAL ENTITIES." My next essay was on G. E. Moore's *Principia Ethica.* He interrupted me again. "But you see, I DO FEEL, I DO FEEL, that Moore did NOT regard GOOD as some sort of THING that you can hand round a DINING ROOM like platefuls of SPAM." MacKinnon's interruptions were famous, I discovered. He was said to have reduced a female freshman to tears when she read her first essay to him. He sat there exclaiming every now and then "Oh dear!" and "Oh how awful!" and sometimes just groaning. The girl faltered, stopped reading, sobbed. MacKinnon sat in silence for a a few minutes, staring at her. Then he boomed: "I MUST SAY, I MUST SAY, that my INTERJECTIONS were not in any way connected with the QUALITY OF YOUR ESSAY. They were occasioned by the fact that I HAVE A TOOTHACHE." MacKinnon was great entertainment, an eccentric in the Oxford tradition. As a tutor he provoked rather than explained. I couldn't always follow him, but then, I thought, I wouldn't expect to be on net with an Anglo-Catholic Socialist philosopher.

I went just for one term to MacKinnon in Keble for philosophy and to Sherwin-White in St. John's for Greek History. This was because most of the dons in Queen's had been doing war work overseas or in high places in the home civil service and were not all back in harness that first term. They were not an inspiring bunch, I decided, when eventually they took over. In fact, they had become more like civil servants than dons. Gilbert Ryle was said to have described the Provost, Sir Oliver Franks, as "a constitutionally unpuzzled man—one who would regard a riot in the Back Quad as a trend." Certainly they couldn't offer me a sufficient counter-attraction to pubs and girls.

Oxford after Burma meant most of all, I am afraid, not intellectual stimulus but pints and pints of Reading Pale

Ale, hours of darts and shove ha'penny, and occasional teatime sex. When an ex-serviceman's oak was sported at four o'clock in the afternoon the scout could be sure that the privacy was required for reasons unconnected with academic work. I was waiting by the porter's lodge one evening after Hall when two scouts passed me on their way out. "The Back Quad's nothing but a bleeding brothel this term, mate." "Back Quad? The whole bloody college, cock!" One of them was Mike Nelson's scout, so he had a wealth of evidence on which to base his comment. Nelson was waiting for his American fiancée to come to England and in the meantime was keeping his hand, so to speak, in. He picked up his girls at dances in the Carfax Assembly Rooms or out at Headington, reckoning nothing to the sexual potential of female undergraduates. Having danced with a girl at night he invited her for tea the next day. When she arrived she would find she was expected to sit on the mattress which Nelson had dragged from his bedroom and placed in front of the fire in the sittingroom. It was cosier like that, on a cold day, he would tell her. Then he set her to toast a pile of crumpets. He believed strongly in the aphrodisiac effect of buttered crumpets, or of the toasting process, he was never quite sure which it was that did the trick, and claimed to have an almost hundred per cent success rate in the subsequent proceedings. At six o'clock he would leave the girl, locking her in the room because, he warned her, he couldn't risk his scout finding her there; he would only be half an hour, but he had to see his tutor about something important. He then appeared in the Buttery for two or three quick pints, to put more lead in his pencil, as he explained to his cronies. Then it was back to the girl for a second round of sex, instead of going into Hall for dinner. After that he would escort her as far as the College Gate, rarely further. When she had departed he was ready for the evening pub crawl. This invariably started in The Eastgate, the nearest pub to Queen's. Sometimes we advanced up the High, via The Wheatsheaf and The Mitre, to White's, a raffish bar near Carfax where American G.I.s took their camp followers. Later, Ken Tynan used to appear there, cloaked and escorting some exotic girl. Another popular route was by The King's Arms and The Turf, and a little pub by Blackwell's, to The Lamb and Flag and The Bird and Baby. Nelson was a small man and became overloaded with beer quite soon. He had the ability to come out of one pub, be copiously sick in the gutter, and then walk across the road and start on more pints in the next pub. The evenings usually finished, after closing time, with a meal of curry and rice, or because it was even cheaper a dish called 'English Vegetables', in the Taj Mahal in the Turl.

My first attempt to emulate Nelson was not an unqualified success. I had noticed a pretty blonde girl attending some of the Greats lectures. Girls reading Greats were unattractive on the whole. There was one we christened Blossom, for her cow-like gait; also, she wore a funny little toque-like hat with two upturned ends like a cow's horns. She always carried a small suitcase, no doubt stuffed with lecture notes. I only went to eleven o'clock lectures, those at ten being too early and those at noon coinciding with the beginning of the lunchtime beer drinking. Blossom, however, always rushed in late, at a fast bovine amble, having obviously come from an earlier lecture, and at twelve rushed away just as fast and clumsily for her graze in some third academic pasture. Compared with girls like that the blonde appeared outstanding. One morning she was among those listening to a man called Hignett who lectured on Greek History in Exeter or Lincoln, I can't remember which. Hignett lectured slowly, ponderously, at dictation speed, as if expecting his audience to note down every word. In the course of a rather dreary exposition of social and political developments in pre-Periclean Athens, he declaimed: "Cleisthenes . . . devised a means . . . of increasing the population . . . without friction." I laughed. The blonde laughed too, and looked across at me. Her reaction showed a higher degree of sexual sophistication than was common among the women undergraduates I had met. After the lecture I asked her to come and have a drink in The Eastgate. She had a gin and tonic. She was Australian. Her name was Cathy Capper. I invited her to tea the following day.

I bought half a dozen crumpets at Marks and Spencers in the Cornmarket and a packet of Durex at a chemist's in the High. Before I left The Eastgate at lunchtime I bought a bottle of gin, too. Nelson's formula might not work in every case, I thought. In front of the fire I upturned my sofa so that its back became a low seat a few inches off the floor. I hung my jacket over a chair so placed that I could extract a French letter from the pocket without having to get up. The fire glowed. The scene was set.

Cathy admired my room and walked all round it. She jumped up on to one of the window seats and jumped down again, putting her hands on my shoulders to steady herself. She asked to see the bedroom, and admired that. At last I got her in position, toasting. It was warm work, she said; she took off the thick sweater she was wearing over a thin yellow blouse. When I brought in the kettle from the gas ring on the staircase I closed the oak. Cathy's conversation was startling. During the second crumpet she told me she had been fitted for a contraceptive. She wore it all the time, she said. "Are you wearing it now?" I asked. "Oh yes," she said, "of course." Of course! She must, I reasoned, be as keen as I was. Nevertheless, there was something rather odd about the direct way in which she had given me the information. It had been done in a naive more than a sophisticated manner, even if it had shown a commendable preoccupation with matters of sex. Could she be a nymphomaniac? I had always wanted to meet one. I moved the débris and began a little preliminary kissing. She responded with enthusiasm and took off her bra. When I licked her nipples she closed her eyes and said "Oh, oh, lovely!" I stroked her thighs, played with her pubic hair, fingered the way in. She wriggled in what I assumed was ecstasy, gasped "Oh, oh, oh!", and then suddenly removed my hand and collapsed in tears. I couldn't understand it. Had I hurt her? Couldn't have. Nor did I think I had gone far enough to satisfy her, even though I now knew a girl could have an orgasm without being penetrated. I could only assume that this was a case of post-coital tristitia without the coitus. She stopped crying as suddenly as she had started, and apologised quite brightly, as if she had committed some social faux pas like knocking over a sugar bowl. "Sorry," she said, "so sorry. It's not your fault." "That's all right," I said, although it wasn't. I was most uncomfortable. She noticed. "Do let me relieve you. Have you got a handkerchief? Or shall I get a towel!" Whether she suggested the alternative merely because she thought I didn't have a handkerchief on me or because she was revising her estimate of the results of the operation she had offered to perform, I did not know. In any case, it struck me as being too like a nurse asking a patient if he wanted a bedpan, and I refused her services. We talked for about half an hour, she brightly, I grumpily. In the course of this I discovered she was married, to an instructor at a physical training college. I decided I wouldn't try again. I introduced her on the way out to a friend on the same staircase. He was still going out with her months later, but he would never tell me what sort of a relationship he had established.

There were, I suppose, about fifty of us in Queen's who had returned from the War. Our priorities were drink and sex, and since for the most part those undergraduates who had come up straight from school placed nothing like the same importance on those two activities we mixed little with them. I have always considered the Aesthete/Hearty classification misleading to describe the many different types and individuals there always were at Oxford, but if it is taken as a scale I expect it would be true to say that I had been somewhere in the Aesthete half during my first year in '39/'40 and now had moved nearer to the Hearty end. And yet the people whose company I now frequented were by no means Hearties through and through: rakes, perhaps, if one wanted to be kind, boors or Philistines if one didn't. We liked games, but those who were in the running for a Blue were not prepared to give up their dissipated way of life long enough to make sure of the distinction. Bob Botha, for example, played for the University XV in their first five matches, but the time he spent in The Eastgate and at late-night poker parties in college was beginning to tell. Newton-Thompson, the captain and, like Bob, a South African, asked him to give up the flesh-pots until after Twickenham. Bob refused, was dropped, and missed his Blue. Bob was the only Boer I ever liked. He had had a chequered career during the War and for a time had been in hospital with DTs in Addis Ababa. He had a sense of humour and a tolerance which did not generally characterise his compatriots. Some of his acquaintances were unspeakably nasty; Nicky Princeloo and one or two others thought no evening's drinking was complete until they had thrown a waiter downstairs or indulged in physical violence of some sort. We told Bob what we thought of them and he didn't invite them to join us again.

No wonder the Queen's dons didn't like us. Those of us who were Scholars must have looked as if we were frittering away any chance of doing well in Schools. John Cummin, a Scholar also reading Greats, dedicated even more time than the rest of us to beer and sex. He was a big, earthy character from Norfolk and had been a Corporal in the Engineers. He carried a bit of a chip on his shoulder because he had not been commissioned and told more war stories than anyone else, most of them designed to show his toughness and the vital role he had played, because of, rather than despite, his rank, in the crossing of the Rhine; he seemed to have been for ever soaked to the skin building bridges in sub-zero temperatures. However, he was a huge success with the girls. Oddly enough, the kind of girl he most attracted was the well brought up English rose. It was surmised that they picked him, or allowed him to pick them, because he was so different from the kind of man with whom they would inevitably settle down; marriage with Cummin was so obviously out of the question that they could have a relaxed sexual fling before mating with their stockbrokers and barristers and going to live in Guildford. He didn't always find it handed to him on a plate, though. Then he would work at 'getting his end away' with the same grim determination he must have shown at forcing other passages when he wore his Corporal's stripes. Sometimes in The Eastgate he issued sitreps on the progress of his current campaign, sometimes he merely hinted that difficult operations were going on but gave no more detailed information until he was able to announce a victory. He arrived once in my room and asked to borrow a pair of underpants. He had been out to tea with a girl in Iffley whose inhibitions he had not yet broken down and he had come so many times in his pants that he had had to throw them away. I asked why he couldn't just put on another pair of his own. It had been the same every day for a week, he said; he hadn't any clean ones left. He was known as Always Cummin after that.

David Edwards had been wounded in the head and was almost blind. His parents were teetotal, and at home in the vacations he had to conceal the smell of beer by chewing parsley on his way back from the pub. For this reason he always drank even more than usual during the last day or two of term, and held a final party in the bar on Oxford Station, insisting that the beer tasted better there because it was served in china mugs. After one of these occasions he got into the train and went straight into a drunken sleep. He woke up when the train stopped, got his bags off the rack and stumbled out into a taxi. "Number twelve, Collingham Gardens," he said. "But that's in Earls Court, isn't it?" "Yes, so what?" "Well, this is Reading," "That's all right. Drive on." This bravado cost him eight pounds, he told us the next term.

George Stockpit came from Staffordshire. He was married, but concealed this successfully both from the dons and from his girl friend, Clarissa. After he went down, having failed to get anything better than a Pass Degree, he was divorced, married Clarissa, a big, rosy-cheeked, sweet-tempered hockey Blue, and opened a prep school near his home. He was the most indiscriminate womanizer I ever met, and his technique varied between the most blatant flattery and the cruellest of insults. He even paid for sex at times, if the price was low enough. One night he flung gravel up at Botha's window. We looked out into the High. Stockpit had one arm round a squat, unsavoury-looking ATS Lance-Corporal. He gave an obscene giggle. "She's half a crown a throw now," he announced. "Was five bob when I had her, but she's half price after midnight. Wish I'd known. Anyway, I don't want her again. Any takers up there?" We were drinking and playing cards, and one look at the Lance-Corporal was enough for us to decide that poker, not poking, was the better bet.

I met a large German girl who lived in a flat in the Turl, two floors above the Taj. I had a barren relationship with her, although she did succeed in taking me to hear a string quartet in Balliol. Her flat was conveniently central, there was that to be said for her; so many girls seemed to live nearer Woodstock or Iffley than Oxford. She liked being fondled to music, preferably Brahms, but would never take off all her clothes and would never agree to what she called "fock ink". She lay on her divan, in piles of cushions, knees up, clothes unbuttoned and half off, humming to her favourite Fourth Symphony on the gramophone, while I toiled up and down and around her, to little purpose. It was too boring to last long, but I feared that her recriminations, when I told her it was all over, would be even more boring. I arranged therefore, that one night at nine o'clock I would tell her I was not going to see her again, there was Someone Else, and at precisely three minutes past nine, before she could get into her stride, Stockpit and Cummin would bang on the door and demand my help in getting a drunken Nelson out of the Taj before he was arrested. The charade was played with meticulous timing and enthusiastic acting—if, indeed, Nelson was acting—and I never saw Inge again.

I decided after a couple of terms that the life I was leading in Oxford was too enjoyable for me to consider modifying it until much nearer the time of Final Schools. On the other hand, my tutor had told me that I could be in the running for a First and I didn't want to rule myself out entirely. I compromised by working really hard at home in the vacations, keeping up an average of nine hours' work a day, including weekends. The only relaxation I allowed myself was to spend the last of each day's licensing hours in the Armitage Arms with my father. My parents were most helpful about this austere way of life, leaving me uninterrupted until it was time to summon me to a meal and accepting without comment that as soon as I had finished eating I would get up and go back to my books. Their own fathers and most male relatives were mining engineers, and they had no direct interest themselves in what interested me; nevertheless, they had always encouraged me, and never tried to divert me, from the time I first went on to the classical side at school. My father had once been upset by my low marks in physics and chemistry and had tried to explain to me, with diagrams, the principle of the internal combustion engine, but for a long time now he had been resigned to what he no doubt regarded as my eccentric tastes and preferences. I don't think my mother minded what I read and wrote so long as I didn't get my feet wet and always had enough to eat. Both of them, indeed, for as long as I could remember, had held strong views about how to preserve good health. Wet feet and sitting in a draught were to be avoided at all costs. They each had their pet remedies for constipation, which they defined as "missing a day", my father being "a big believer in" Carter's Little Liver Pills, my mother favouring a black, glutinous paste called Prunol. Every cut and graze called for a liberal application of iodine. At the first sign of a sore throat you gargled with glycerine of thymol. And my mother had strictly forbidden me ever to buy ice cream from a 'Stop Me and Buy One' vehicle; she had never explained specifically what she thought might happen if I disobeyed her, and for a long time I had believed that the appearance of the 'fever van' was in some way related to the previous activities of Walls and Eldorado ice cream pedlars. My parents worried now about the liklihood of my working too hard and having a "nervous breakdown", but they accepted my assurances without serious protest and did not try to break me from the discipline.

Back in Oxford in term time I did the minimum of work needed to write passable essays. So far as I could observe, that sort of régime was not uncommon among undergraduates who had returned from the War, but the Press had got it into their heads that we were all much more serious and hardworking than either the 'jeunesse dorée' of before the War or those coming up now straight from school. That view was just about as accurate as the current one that students are mainly junkies, layabouts or professional demonstrators.

What ought to have worried me if I had looked at myself and considered my behaviour (which I never did) was that in 1945–47 I took no part in University politics, wrote nothing for any of the magazines, joined no societies except a College dining club. The War should have been no more than a parenthesis. Instead, I had allowed it to alter the plot and affect character. I was leading a different kind of life because I had become a different sort of person with a different, or at least distorted, set of values. Pleasure and survival had become the important things to aim at. Survival during the War had meant not being killed. Now it meant doing as little work as necessary to obtain a respectable degree that would help me to acquire a lucrative job. Pleasure in Burma had meant having enough rum and sleeping with boots off. In Oxford it meant eight to ten pints of bitter most nights and a girl and buttered crumpets every now and then at tea time. In a war so much that is important is 'given', either decided by others or as fortuitous and beyond control as the weather. You become accustomed to exercising choice only in less important matters, in means rather than ends. You settle for alleviating, not transforming, the environment. As a result, not only in immediately post-War Oxford but ever since, I have tended to give little thought to big questions like where to live, how many children to have, and whether to change my job. It is as if the campaign strategy for life had already been laid down; decisions for me to take were only of the same order as the siting of slit trenches and the timing of the next hot meal. I know I appear to be blaming the War for what is obviously an inherent defect in my character. I think though that this defect was accentuated and nourished by the War and might not have been so operative if my time from the age of 20 to 25 had been spent in quite other circumstances. On the credit side, I suppose, is the fact that in moments of depression I can think back to when I would have settled for anything so long as pieces of jagged metal were not flying around in the air nearby; most things seem better in the light of that sort of remembrance of time past.

When I approached the University Appointments Committee in 1947 I hankered after a job which would involve writing, but my brief to them was largely negative. I was reading Greats, I said, and was held to stand some chance of a First, but I didn't want to teach or go into the Civil Service. They suggested publishing, advertising or journalism, and arranged three interviews. The first was with Geoffrey Faber, who was a Fellow of All Souls. He was far from encouraging. Most publishing houses were family businesses. Furthermore, there was a shortage of paper, and anything where the printing of words was concerned, not just publishing but advertising and journalism too, was unable to expand and take on new staff; they were hard pushed to find places for their own pre-War people now returning and wanting their jobs back. For his part, he thought I had perhaps been too quick to rule out teaching. The second interview was with the managing director of a big London advertising agency. I hadn't known that there were such things as advertising agencies; I'd assumed that there just happened to be a chap in Guinness's brewery who had a nice turn of wit and was handy with a paintbrush, and that most other firms were not so lucky. When I discovered from the Appointments Committee that there were people in these agencies who were paid—and paid quite highly if they made the grade—to produce slogans and write copy for products like Guinness, Bovril and Colman's Mustard, it struck me as a pleasant way to survive in the world of careers and moneymaking. However, having gone sober and dark-suited to the off-putting conversation with Faber, I decided I'd go tweeded and full of beer to see the advertising man. A shot in the dark like that might be more likely to hit the target, I reasoned.

It did. I hadn't worked out what to say, but inspired by my lunchtime intake of Reading Pale Ale I talked a lot about the effectiveness of puns and why "Did you Maclean your teeth today?" was such a good slogan. I liked the man who interviewed me. He was the son of Robert Bevan, the painter, and had been a Captain in the Navy during the War. He was a more entertaining talker than Faber. He urged the importance of adding "a touch of corroborative detail to an otherwise bald and unconvincing narrative". When he wrote to offer me a job as a trainee copywriter I accepted straightaway. However, I still went to the third interview. It was with Tom Hopkinson, editor of *Picture Post*. This was before Hulton began sacking his editors every few months. Hopkinson offered me a job, too, and it sounded more attractive than copywriting. One week, he told me, I might be sent to Germany to see how a badly bombed town was recovering, the next to Italy to watch a film director at work, the third to cover a day in the life of a surgeon in a London teaching hospital. I refused his offer, with some reluctance, and stuck to the one I had accepted. This was partly because I had already written to Bevan to accept, but chiefly, I suspect, because I had an idea that in advertising I was likely to earn more money and get on the board of the company more quickly than in journalism, And Bevan looked more prosperous than Hopkinson.

No doubt I should have weighed copywriting against reporting to decide which was 'better', whatever that meant (more dignified? more socially useful?), but it never occurred to me to make that sort of value judgment. Essays were all I'd written at Oxford since the War, not a single short story or review, and it had become progressively harder to force myself out of the pubs and into a cinema or theatre. One week I had tried to see a film at the Scala Cinema in Walton Street. Unfortunately, as you approached the cinema you came to a pub called The Jericho and on its sign was the invitation, "Tarry a While". It was an invitation my companion and I had accepted three times that week, never getting to see the film. I was in no mood to make a considered choice between the jobs offered me. Going into advertising was like dropping into a pub, and I "tarried" there, not merely in the advertising business, but actually in the same agency, for twenty-two years.

Most of us in our last two terms had pulled ourselves together, pub crawled a little less often and worked several hours a day. A few were so demoralised that they found even this self-discipline beyond them. They mooched sheepishly round the College in the afternoons, playing shove ha'penny in the JCR, trying vainly to get enough of their old drinking companions together for a "session". Cummin, as a result, got such a bad degree that the only job he could find was farm labouring. The last time we all drank together was some weeks after the end of our final term, when we were called back to Oxford for our vivas. We gathered in The Eastgate at about six o'clock. At half past, Jess, the College messenger before the War and porter afterwards, came in and stood in front of me. He looked fierce. "Not more than three or four pints tonight, John. You're being viva-ed for a First tomorrow." Jess's information was nearly always accurate, so I drank only two pints before Hall and two—well, three, actually—after. My viva the next morning lasted almost an hour and a half. I stuck to my position as a logical positivist, firing shots in the dark from my Ayer gun, but I felt my defences crumbling towards the end. I went straight into The Eastgate, sweating. My tutor came into the bar a bit later to tell me that they had given me a First. He was one of the examiners, but because I was his pupil he had had to leave the room while I was being interrogated. When he was recalled, he told me, it was in time to hear the chief examiner say doubtfully: "Well, at least he TALKS like a philosopher." That summed it up, I think. I had 'survived'. But it was cunning, not scholarship, that had made me a good enough examinee to creep in among the bottom Firsts. The doubt in the examiner's voice, and his emphasis on "TALKS like", showed that they had nearly rumbled me.

Post Scriptum

All endings are to some extent arbitrary, but it seems to me that 1947 provides a more natural break than any other time I could have chosen. Up to then I had 'belonged' to organisations, a school, a university, an army. In the autumn of that year I took a job in an advertising agency and a month or two later got married. Business and marriage together made a very different way of life from any I had led before. I do not mean that it was either more or less challenging, satisfying, alarming or absurd, but that the challenges, satisfactions, alarms and absurdities were of a different sort and combined to form a different pattern. It's another story, I think, from then on, and that is why *Shots in the Dark* ends where it does.